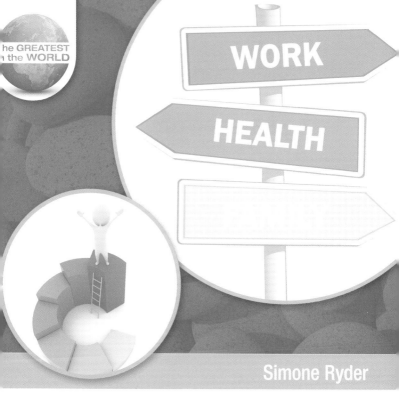

WORK

HEALTH

Simone Ryder

The Greatest
ife Coaching
Tips
in the World

A 'The Greatest in the World' book

www.thegreatestintheworld.com

Cover images:
© Palabra; © Alexey Afanasyev
both courtesy of www.fotolia.com, © Steve Brookes

Layout:
Shazia Saleemi
www.designspirit.co.uk

Copy editor:
Bronwyn Robertson
www.theartsva.com

Series creator/editor:
Steve Brookes

Published in 2008 by
The Greatest in the World Ltd, PO Box 3182,
Stratford-upon-Avon, Warwickshire CV37 7XW

Text and design Copyright © 2008 – The Greatest in the World Ltd

A CIP catalogue record for this book is available from the British Library
ISBN 978-1-905151-23-3

Printed and bound in Italy by Printer Trento s.r.l.

I would like to dedicate this book,
with love, to my daughters
Danielle and Christine

Contents

A few words from Simone...

Wouldn't it be great if there was someone helping you get to the heart of what you really want and encouraging you to take steps to make positive lasting change? Life Coaching is now the most popular way to help people to really take charge of their lives, creating life goals that bring the happiness they so much desire.

This book is written for anyone who wants to feel happy and fulfilled in their life. Whether they are at a crossroads and need to make a big decision or simply doubt what to do next, then they will find inspiration and practical techniques and tools within this book to release their potential, increase their motivation, develop more confidence and create the personal happiness they truly want.

I hope you enjoy the tips in this book and if you only apply some of them to your life, you will be creating a positive change. Remember, obstacles are those frightening things you see when you take your eyes of the goal, so read on, find your passion, challenge yourself, set your life goals and take action.

Good luck!

Simone x

One life

One life, one smile,
many chances for a while.
Once swift and with haste,
time and laughter with no grace.

Work, family and health,
invisible growth and stealth.
Years follow on, questions arise
recalling love and loss demise.

Performing life for another,
a single sheep behind it's mother.
Commit and aim, be your best -
stumble, strive, push on with zest.

Life and grace does not wait
for those that watch dry paint
Look up, climb high, don't be afraid to fall.
Make every moment count, get over that wall.

One life, one smile,
many chances for a while.
Be swift, be hasty
for life is sweet and very tasty.

By Simone Ryder

The past does not equal the future.

Anon

What is life coaching?

WHO WHAT
WHERE
WHY WHEN
& HOW

chapter 1
What is life coaching?

Many people are drawn to life coaching because they feel their life is out of balance. They may be working too hard and have no time left for all the other things they value or they may be going through a big change, in their relationship, career, family, money, health or home, all of which have an unbalancing effect and create fears and feelings of uncertainty. Life coaching helps people to know themselves and what they really want and how to move forward; from this point they can then make decisions with confidence.

Life Coaching originated in the United States and developed out of sport and business coaching, whereby a trained coach would help their sporting athlete or business client to set specific goals and then work alongside them to motivate, encourage and support them to success, using various techniques and motivational tools to help them gain progress. The coach would also help their client break past any negative beliefs that they may have about their ability, which might be holding them back.

It's not just about goals – it's taking action

Using a life coach helps you to structure your daily thoughts into a routine, set goals and act daily to achieve them and with a clear agenda, it transforms your mindset and habits into positive action.

What's your attitude?

If you use a life coach to help you set your new agenda for the life you want, then clear and powerful revelations will take place. Negative thought patterns are worked through and eliminated and positive empowering thoughts are created in order for you to quite simply see the wood for the trees, and this will help you to look at your attitude to yourself, your life, your capabilities and what you really want. Adjusting your mindset to a positive 'can do' attitude.

Who needs a life coach?

Many people think life coaching is like a form of counselling or therapy, an opportunity to sit and pour out your problems. However, although life coaching has similarities with therapy, such as listening and helping a person in a non-judgemental and confidential environment, its main objective is to help people know who they are and what they want for their life, help them be true to themselves and take action to change their life in a positive way, with the focus on taking action and motivating the person to move forward.

Focus and breaking through

As with counselling, a life coach will listen and empathise with their client to help them have clarity on their life situation and this will include looking at the issues, behaviour and feelings around the client's current life. However, the life coach will help the client to look beyond this and assist them in setting personal goals, to motivate, inspire and encourage their client to move forward into the life they would like, whilst looking at the impact of any changes they make, breaking through old patterns of behaviour and limiting beliefs that may cause them to feel stuck.

Life coaching may feel a little like a therapy session at times, however, the client should come away with a clear set of actions and should feel motivated to achieve them. Over a period of time the coach will challenge the client to move forward in achieving their goals step by step.

Life coach, mentor, therapist or counsellor?

Mentors

These people are usually an expert in their particular area or job and have lots of experience to help other people in the same field. They will help by listening and then advising and guiding another person over a period of time. An example of this might be a tutor with a student or a senior manager with a new salesperson on their team.

Therapists

There are many types of therapist, sport therapist, art therapist, dance therapist, psychotherapist. A therapist is usually medically trained in their particular field and is skilled at treating emotional or psychological disorders. Another example of this might be a branch of therapy such as hypnotherapy whereby a person will be helped with specific issues, phobias or addictions such as wanting to stop smoking.

Counsellors

Work with people to help them explore a difficulty, feelings of distress, or dissatisfaction in their life. They provide a safe environment, listening to and encouraging clients to think clearly about their situation and perhaps consider a new perspective. Counsellors do not give advice or direct a client to a solution, but help the client to choose freely a way forward by reducing confusion and promoting a better understanding themselves.

Life Coaches

These are upbeat, positive people who work to get the very best out of someone and enabling them to make decisions that will improve their life. Coaches help people to move forward and do not claim to have all the answers. A coach's job is to understand and empathise with their client, which includes understanding the client's background, and then they work with the client to help them find the answers within themselves. This can cover a number of areas, for example: achieving a better work/life balance; feeling more fulfilled at work; improving relationships with family and partners; learning better parenting skills that benefit both the child and parent; gaining a spiritual meaning to life, or a desire to 'get sorted'.

It's a relationship dedicated to you

A life coach is more of a partnership than anything else. It is a support system with one goal in mind: improving your quality of life. Time that you dedicate specifically to yourself to improve your life and your happiness.

What do you want?

A life coach will direct this question to their client in many ways and encourage their client to think hard and deeply about what is most important to them. For many people this is the first time they have been able to be completely honest about what they truly want and as they look at each area of their life, they begin to see patterns of behaviour and experiences that have developed out of not really knowing what they want and following a vague idea of what being happy means to them.

Many people have never taken the time to understand who they are and what they value most in life, considering 'being happy' as enough. However, being happy means very different things to people and when this is looked at more closely the coach can usually see very clearly what the client needs to do or change in order to have a happy life.

It is important to point out here that a life coach does not tell their client what they think; they help the client to find out what they really want by asking probing questions and giving feedback to ensure the client understands what is being said, as this is the only way the client can be truly sure it is they who have discovered what they really want and not a suggestion from someone else. The difficult part for many is getting past the fears that have kept them from making the positive changes already!

What makes a good life coach?

Firstly, training qualifications from a reputable training organisation and a variety of technical coaching skills such as NLP (Neuro Linguistic Programming explained below), can have a beneficial effect in helping the coach to help their clients change negative patterns of behaviour and limiting beliefs about themselves. Secondly a life coach who has many hours of experience in coaching people.

A good life coach is definitely one who walks the talk which is a real strength in a life coach, as they need the ability to really empathise with other people, so the more life experience the life coach has the more they can understand the needs of their clients.

A good life coach is happy, healthy and good to be around, they may also specialise in a certain area, for example parenting skills, well-being, relocation, retirement or spiritual coaching. Life coaches who have personal experience of achieving success in their specialist areas tend to be more passionate, enthusiastic and able in helping others to achieve the same results.

Finding the right life coach for you?

The best way to hire a great life coach is through personal recommendation from someone you know and then you can actually see the living proof from the success of the coaching they received. However, if you need to start from scratch in choosing a life coach, researching the Internet for a life coach in your area is a good place to start; line up at least three or four and give them a call for a chat or arrange to meet them face to face if you can.

A good life coach will be happy to do this and understand your need to talk or meet them first; these initial meetings are usually free of charge and informal. If your coach has not come with a recommendation, then ask the life coach to show you their qualifications and testimonials from previous clients and ask them how many coaching hours they have done with clients.

Asking questions – choosing with confidence

The best way to judge whether you will be able to get on and trust this person as your life coach is to ask them questions about who they have coached before and what successes they have had. Explain a little about your need to have a life coach and ask how they would be able to help you; ask if you can call a couple of their past clients for a recommendation and this will give you more confidence in choosing. It's also worth pointing out that we all have different personalities, so find a coach who you feel really empathises with you and makes you feel comfortable about being yourself and yet with enough assertiveness to challenge you too!

What techniques do life coaches use

Mainly experience and personality, however, life coaches are trained to use different tools and techniques to help you identify your goals, help you to look at what you value and how your beliefs can influence how you feel about your abilities and choices in life. The various techniques used help the coach to get inside your thoughts and find out where you are coming from; from this point they are more able to ask the right questions in order to help you see exactly who you are and why you think the way you do about your life. This is a very important part of life coaching, because it is from this point that the client can become clear about making decisions.

NLP (Neuro Linguistic Programming) is a technique used by some life coaches and is believed to bring about change by taking back the control of one's own mind. This is done by applying three principles:

Neuro – the nervous system which processes and codes information into our memory.

Linguistic – the language pattern of the individual and how we communicate on a verbal level with other people or with the use of symbols such as writing words, numbers or drawings, and the neural processes of the mind.

Programming – this is the coding arrangement of the two previous elements which provides us with the means to put in order our sensors, such as our sight, smell, touch, hearing, and verbal to create new and successful behaviour patterns

The power of music

A certain piece of music can put you straight into a good mood, the brain will remember how you felt happy when you heard that music and experienced something happy in the past. The same is true of sad experiences, music is very powerful at influencing our feelings and it will recall those feelings fast, so next time you want to feel positive and upbeat, but on your favourite tune and notice how the brain immediately changes state.

"

A belief is a
preconceived attitude
based on the past. "

Richard Wilkins

How does this NLP work in coaching?

It's all about creating winning patterns in the mind, which produce positive habits and patterns of behaviour. NLP takes the old patterns (which may have been negative and self doubting) and creates new patterns, which gives the person more control over how they feel and see their world and their abilities.

Therefore, life coaches who have training in NLP to become a practitioner, will use their knowledge gained from understanding the principles of NLP to help them understand their clients more deeply; they are able to use these techniques to benefit their clients in getting past limiting beliefs and help them to break through old patterns when they have felt blocked and unable to change the way they think.

NLP provides a different perspective on the expression of life — for example some of the expressions a coach may use when they want to get their client to think about making positive changes:

1. If what you are doing is not working, do something else.

2. People already have all the resources they need inside their minds.

3. The meaning of your communication is the response that you get.

4. The mind and the body are parts of the same system.

5. People always make the best choices available to them.

One person's experience of NLP...

To give you just one simple example of how NLP works, a lady had wanted to lose weight for several years and talked about it a lot, tried various diets and genuinely did not like feeling overweight and unhealthy; she caught a glance of herself in a shop window and felt shocked that she looked that way, as she felt she was a different person on the outside from how she felt she looked on the inside.

The lady decided to get fit and stop eating junk food, she had 4 stone to lose and so she talked to a life coach about why she wanted to do this. She wanted to have more energy, feel more confident and live longer, and yet during her coaching sessions she discovered that her mind had built a pattern of thinking about food that was attached to her emotions and this had supported her overeating with a negative perception of herself. These feelings were reinforced in the negative way she spoke about herself and this negative belief was stopping her from achieving the success she so wanted in losing weight.

The lady had not realised that she had been programming her mind and body to accept the overeating in order to ignore her real feelings.

Using NLP she looked more deeply into why she had been overeating and why she had tried and failed many times to stop and lose the weight; it became clear to her that she had formed a limiting belief about herself and had become afraid of being her true self, the real her which was slim, confident and in control of her life. This lady began to realise that past experiences which had knocked her confidence, had set up a negative pattern (programme) in her subconscious about her self worth, which she had accepted as the truth!

With her new insight this lady was then able to replace the old pattern of thinking with the one she wanted to experience. Using visualisation to see and experience her life as a success, part of which was losing the weight and getting fit, the lady then started with realistic steps to achieve her goals, keeping her new belief clear in her mind. She went on to lose all the weight and tell her story in this book!

Blended coaching

Many people with existing skills of working with others are now becoming trained in coaching skills and techniques to enhance their ability to bring out the best in themselves and others. Many life coaches often use their life experience to focus on a specific field of coaching in which they have had personal experience, such as Parent coaching, Stress Management coaching, Health and Well-being coaching. However, more and more professional and highly trained individuals in other jobs now benefit from gaining coaching skills. These skills are blended together and provide very useful tools and techniques to bring out the best in their work environment, personal work performance and enhance the success of those they help through their work already.

Teachers, doctors and police are just a few examples where extra coaching skills blended together with key work skills increase the benefit to those they have to communicate with and work to help.

Summary

- A great life coach is passionate about life and is someone who inspires you and 'walks the talk'.

- When you have life coaching, focusing on what you value will help you to understand what is most important to you.

- Coaching may seem like therapy sometimes, but you should get clear goals, motivation and a plan of action.

- Time with your coach is about you taking 100% responsibility for improving your life and personal happiness.

- Setting goals for your life is one of the most liberating and exciting things you can do to improve it.

- Life coaching reveals the patterns of your behaviour and how they may limit your personal success and confidence.

- Clarify your 'purpose in life' through coaching and you will find that your passion and motivation for life will increase.

- Ideally get a recommendation for a great coach, alternatively line up three or four coaches to talk to before you choose your personal coach.

- Personality and an ability to empathise with you is necessary for a good life coach to understand what you need and want, and then help you move forward.

- NLP techniques are a way to help you overcome limiting patterns of behaviour that may be stopping you from achieving personal success; visualisation is one element of NLP.

Change a **can't** to a **could** and you've got a **chance**.

Anon

Embracing change

chapter 2
Embracing change

One thing we can all be sure of is that life will keep presenting us with challenges and our lives will go through a continual cycle of change. However, most people don't enjoy too much change, it upsets the flow of life and generally we like to know that things are the same from one day to the next; it gives us a sense of security and continuity in our lives. So it's no surprise that when we have to face some difficult challenges in life and changes that come along from time to time, it can cause us to feel insecure and out of control and we really don't like the feeling of too much uncertainty.

Some changes we choose and in doing so inflict a sense of unease and uncertainty in our lives, because it excites us and we feel it will be a good or great change with all the feelings that will come with it; getting married is a good example!

However, there are many things that come as a shock to our lives too, and when change is unplanned it can be derailing for our emotions and can take time to adjust.

Let's take a look at just some of the areas in life that create challenge for us and the changes we have to adapt to.

Challenging areas of change

1. Moving to a new home.
2. Getting engaged or married.
3. Getting divorced or splitting from a long term partner!
4. Having a baby or becoming a step-parent.
5. Starting a new job.
6. Dating again after divorce.
7. New systems or new boss at work.
8. Becoming unemployed.
9. 40th birthday or any other birthday for that matter!
10. Living in a different country.
11. Bringing up a young family.
12. Getting and looking older!
13. Health problems.
14. Looking after elderly parents.
15. Losing someone close.
16. Retirement.
17. Meeting the love of your life!
18. Winning the lottery!
19. Grown up kids leaving the home (nest).
20. Starting your own business.

Wow! The list is endless, but the reality is that we are challenged daily with change; sometimes it is out of choice and we want that change and know it will be a challenge but it feels positive. However, other times change is thrust upon us or even creeps up without us seeing it and—bang!—it feels like such a shock and so unexpected, it can really upset the balance of our life.

Becoming aware of the change

Once you know something has changed in your life it can throw you into a state of shock to start with and for some time it might be difficult to make sense of what has happened. If you have gone through this, then take a moment to think about a time when something changed in your life and the feelings you went through until you adjusted to the change.

For many people they feel a sense of shock and then a mixture of feelings depending on what the change is; the key to moving through change and coping with it effectively is to first be aware of what is happening and allow the feelings to be acknowledged, then move forward into finding a way out of any negative feelings into a more positive state.

Now write down what changes you are going through in your life today and how these are challenging you:

....

....

....

....

First steps to change

The first steps to coping with change are acknowledging what is happening and how you honestly feel about it; so let's take a look at your challenges and what has changed or is changing in your life that you want to focus on. I now want you to acknowledge how you really feel about it and it will help you to write these feelings down in your notes or circle the words below that you think describe how you feel. Don't be surprised if you feel a mixture of positive and negative feelings all together!

Scared	Worried	Excited
Angry	Resentful	Lonely
Depressed	Sad	Confused
Insecure	Happy	Secure
Anxious	Restless	Calm
Quiet	Relaxed	Motivated
Lost	Confident	Stressed
Positive	Negative	Enthusiastic
Out of control	Agitated	Carefree

OK great – so take a look at what you have acknowledged and accept that this is how you feel and that whatever it is, this is the real you right now. The next question that always comes up in life coaching: What are you going to do about it? Do you want to stay like this or do you want it to change? And if you want it to change then this is the point at which you can honestly start to look at your options of how to move forward into feeling more positive and in control again.

Moving on through change

If change is something we can't stop, then learning to live with change and accepting that it will keep happening will help us to move with change quicker and adjust in order to find happiness and balance in our lives again. For some people they hold onto how they wanted their life to be before a big change came along and feel unable to move forward. For some people it may feel somehow that moving on will mean letting go of a certain level of control they feel in hanging on to the past, however this is a false belief and whilst they are busy looking backwards at the old times they are missing out on their future. Sometimes this is hard to do.

The truth is that when you have something that makes you happy and secure you want to hold on to that, it makes sense for us not to want to cause difficulty in our lives. However, when change comes along and it means letting go of this, then the more important this security is—whether it be a job, a person, a home, an age—the more you don't want to lose it. But ask yourself "Do I really have what I had before?". Admit to yourself that change has happened and that you have found it hard to accept – until now!

The second thing is to understand just how important this change has been to you and what it means to your life. You have done this by circling all the emotions you feel about this change and that will show you just how important and significant this is to you. This is important, don't ignore it and pretend it doesn't matter: it does. It's your life and you matter!

In a cycle of continual change?

It helps to imagine change as a cycle of emotions and activities, so that you can see where you are in relation to this. Where are you in this cycle? Take a look and identify with where you feel you are right now.

Step 1
A change happens – a big or a small shock which could be any number of things.

Step 2
You experience a whole range of emotions and often shock and disbelief followed by either positive or negative emotions, depending on what it was.

Step 3
Generally a positive shock will mean that you will adjust and feel happy and positive quickly and although apprehensive about the change or challenges to come, you may feel able to cope and look forward to the future and imagine ways in which you will learn to embrace this change. Getting married, having a baby, or a big promotion with a lot of responsibility would be a good example of this!

However, a negative shock might be harder to adjust to and feelings of confusion and being out of control may cause anxiety, anger, resentment, and then possibly sadness and real grief for something or someone who was always there and is now gone without you feeling prepared for that change.

Step 4
Feeling low and sad and out of control about the change in your life can leave you feeling stuck and overwhelmed and if

it's been a particular change causing a big shock, then you may feel like this for a long time. But how long you continue to feel like this can be addressed and there will come a time when you want to move forward again.

Step 5

The important element to see in the cycle of change is that being stuck in a place of sadness and not being happy is not what your life is about; you have so much to give and live and love for, so finding your way out of this state will bring you good feelings and is the way forward. This is where you accept the change and decide the only way out is up again! Having acknowledged your feelings and then made a decision to feel good again it's time to focus on **HOW.**

Step 6

Moving on from the change into the future takes courage, but as soon as you begin to take action to change your life for the better you will begin to feel the positive effects. From this point on **the change is no longer controlling you and how you feel – YOU are back in control** and have decided to feel better, more positive and get back to living with a positive outlook and ready for the next challenge that life will throw at you.
Now for **ACTION!**

Now you have acknowledged where you are on the cycle of change – **YOU CAN** do something about it now, and writing down your feelings, as you did above, and then what you will start to do to change them is the step up again to positive feelings. Take a moment now to write down one action that will move you through this cycle and back in control again.

"Everything changes
when YOU change.

Anon

Write down what that action is, what you need to do and when you are going to do it!

....

....

....

....

....

....

....

....

....

....

....

....

....

Brilliant! Now just go and do it – what have you got to lose?!

What if...

Now is a good time to look at the what if question. It may be a good change that you wanted to happen, but it may also be a change that you didn't expect and you didn't see coming. Either way it's happened, so how do you deal with it positively and move forward again?

Ask yourself this question…

What if I stay as I am now and feel like this in one month's time? What will my life be like? Will my feelings affect my family, my health, my job, my friends?

Write your answer here:

....
....
....
....
....
....

What if I stay as I am now and feel like this in six months' time? What will my life be like? Will my feelings affect my family, my health, my job, my friends?

Write your answer here:

....
....
....
....
....
....

What if I accept responsibility for my own feelings and decide to do something positive to help myself move on, how will that help me and what effect will that have on my feelings in one month's time? What will my life be like? Will my feelings affect my family, my health, my job, my friends?

Write your answer here:

....

....

....

....

....

What if I accept responsibility for my own feelings and decide to do something positive to help myself move on, how will that help me and what effect will that have on my feelings in six months' time? What will my life be like? Will my feelings affect my family, my health, my job, my friends?

Write your answer here:

....

....

....

....

....

So now you know that ACTION is very important if you are going to make a positive change and move forward; but also using this exercise whenever you face a change in your life will help you to make sense of what you feel, what you need and how you need to start taking positive action to move forward again instead of feeling stuck and overwhelmed.

How to embrace change

Would you feel more confident and positive about your life if you knew that no matter what happened to you, no matter what big or small changes lay around the corner ready to jump out and surprise you, you would be able to cope with them, that you would be able to accept them with it no matter how hard, and move forward again? The answer lies in being aware of who you are and what is going on in your life. If you put your head in the sand when something is going wrong in your life or making you feel unhappy and uncomfortable, then that is the time to see it for what it is and not be afraid to be honest with yourself. At this crucial moment of awareness, it is time to look at what may be happening and what will happen if you don't address it now – you can feel in control of change if you stay prepared.

An example of confronting fear/change

A relationship that has gone off the boil and neither one of the couple is prepared to say what they really feel is the issue, something has changed between them, but they put their heads in the sand and carry on regardless, for the sake of the children, for appearances sake or any other reason/excuse they give themselves! But both are unhappy and regularly get irritated and angry or resentful with each other. So whatever has happened between them has been ignored (**not acknowledged**) and therefore they can't even begin to be **honest about their feelings** about themselves or each other, and so they go on and on until they feel beyond irritated and resentful and become sad, desperate, unconnected and overwhelmed with the change that has happened to them. Now you can see that by moving through the cycle of change and being aware that it happens will give you confidence to embrace change without fear, because you know that you will find a way forward when you acknowledge honestly what you feel and need.

Worry and fear stop action

We live in a worry culture, filled with fears, stress, tension, nervousness! If you often agitate over things that might go wrong, you may well be plagued by worry. Firstly you need to be aware that you do this in order to release the emotion of worry, notice the part of your body it most frequently inhabits. Don't judge yourself for worrying, but make friends with it, what does it feel like and sound like, so that you know when it's around. You might realise that being a person who worries so much may be an old habit connected to your past when it signified caring, soothing or sympathy for someone important in your life. By investing your energy in worrying for all the right reasons, it has now become a negative habit without you realising.

So ask yourself, what purpose does this serve me now today? Is it really showing caring and comfort and sympathy to others or is it actually in control of me, and if I continue to worry, how is this going to affect my future?

Let go of the worry and anxiety for what it was and replace it with something positive you would like to feel, so for example when you know you would normally worry about something and get agitated, do something to make yourself laugh, this ignites happiness and positive feelings. People who worry tend to take themselves seriously and close down to fun and enjoyment which just makes anxiety levels even worse.

Practise laughter, go to a laughter workshop or watch a funny movie and have a good belly laugh!

Moving out of the comfort zone!

So let's say you acknowledge the change and how you feel about it and want to change this in a positive way; you even know what to do and there is nothing stopping you, then you hear that little voice of worry or the little voice of fear saying "You'd better not do that because it might not work" or "If you do that it might be worse" or even "Don't bother, you know it won't make any difference"! Any of that sound familiar?

That's the little voice everyone has which in essence helps our self-preservation, but it also keeps us stuck in a comfort zone because nobody likes to fail. If you make a decision to change the way you feel and be positive, you have to challenge yourself not to give in to the doubting voice and take a small step that doesn't feel like a massive risk and then another and then another, before you know it, you've done it – you have moved out of that comfort zone!

Face it – life is a challenge

There are times in life when we feel like it is all an uphill struggle; people say things like "It never rains but it pours" and "Bad things all seem to happen at once"! However, we can progress through the challenges of life when we accept that life is a struggle, it will not be all sweetness and light, things will go wrong and life is a constant flow of change. So before you get downhearted let's take this insight and turn it into something positive...

Learn to accept

Adapt to the challenges in life by reminding yourself of the positive things you do have in your life no matter what is happening to you, so when things are good look around and be grateful and when things get tough take a moment and write down a list of positives that will still exist in your life. It may feel strange to do this when you feel down because your brain will be in a negative state and won't be focusing on anything good, so this is where you need to help yourself by providing your brain with some reminders.

Get out the photos of happy times you would like to remember, go through your qualifications or read your CV. Go to a place that always makes you feel good because you had good times there or put that piece of music on that always brings a smile to your face. Remember your brain can be tricked into thinking it's happy and positive even when change is happening – you just have to give it the right information and it will remember happy times!

Take a note – keep a diary!

It makes a big difference if you write down and keep note of how you feel when life is challenging you. Make a point of making positive comments on your day or thoughts no matter how bad things get, as it's proven that writing down our thoughts, ideas and goals are 80% more effective that just thinking or talking about them.

Connect thoughts and feelings

When you make a note in your diary or just write down on a bit of paper or on your PC your thoughts about the day, it may help you to focus, relax and move forward. It doesn't matter if negative things have happened, the questions will help your mind assess the truth of what you are thinking and work out a solution.

What have I done today for myself? ....

....

What have I done today for another person? ....

....

What have I learnt about myself today? ....

....

....

How can I be my best tomorrow? What do I need to do? ....

....

....

Summary

- Your success is determined by how you deal with change.

- A coach will help you understand your fear of change and give you clarity and choice.

- Writing down times of change in your life will help you to identify the highs and lows.

- If change is something we can't stop, then learning to accept this will help us to maintain and re-balance life.

- The more important someone or something is to us, the harder it is when things change and we hang on and refuse to change. This only holds us back.

- It helps to imagine change as a cycle of emotions, moving through stages and coming out the other side – ready for the next change!

- Don't be stuck in a negative cycle of sadness and unhappiness. Accepting all the emotions of change will help us move on.

- Asking the 'what if' questions helps to understand and become aware of our thoughts and behaviour.

- Worry and fear develop into stress, tension and frustration. Turn worry and fear into positive action.

- Keeping a diary of your goals and feelings is more effective than just talking about them.

Just because they're your beliefs, don't be fooled into thinking that they always act in your best interests.

Anon

Finding your passion

chapter 3
Finding your passion

Life Coaching is not about changing yourself, but rather about becoming yourself, helping you to develop your passion and motivation for the life you want to live!

The more you know about yourself, what you love, what you dislike, what makes you excited, what fills you with a passion for life and what makes you motivated, then the easier it is for you to set goals and achieve what you need in order to be happy.

Feeling motivated to live a life full of passion and happiness is possible when you are honest about who you are and what you really want! But here's the thing, most of us think we know who we are and what we want out of life, wake up and go to bed doing the same things every day and yet as the years go by something seems to change. Our passion for the life we would love to have has declined, we accept our lot, we move into a comfortable place (the comfort zone) and settle back, no longer wanting to take the risk to be who we really are. But why does this happen?

The word NO stops passion!

Children are enthusiastic and motivated to learn, to survive and grow, it is a basic instinct. However, as we grow up and begin to understand the world around us, our parents, teachers and peers begin to influence our understanding of who we are, what we can or cannot do and what will happen if we do our own thing and not what they consider to be the right thing! For very good reasons a parent will say no as a child goes to run across a busy road or is in danger.

However, the natural enthusiasm and motivation we are all born with is slowly influenced by the experiences we have, and the most powerful experience we feel is love. So to be loved or liked and wanted, we learn to curb who we are and what we want in order to maintain this emotion or connection. As this emotion is also a basic instinct of survival, it's there inside us for a reason, to keep us together as human beings and maintain the human race. The problem comes when we give up who we are in order to achieve and maintain this love connection; we lose sight of what we may have originally wanted because it became more important to us to feel loved.

Do you know who you are?

So here's the question, if you know who you are, you will know what you value! Do you know what you value and what is most important to you?

We all value things, but what exactly are your life values, the things in life that are very important to you and give you a happy feeling when these values and needs are being met?

The challenge in life is to understand what you value first, this is who YOU are, and then live a life which reflects these values honestly in what you hold most important. This is not easy as some people may feel this is being selfish, however, following what other people value is not being true to yourself.

What do you value the most?

When you know what your personal values are, you will be on track with directing your life forward. Take a moment to write down what you value. I've included some examples and you can circle the ones you think apply to you and add more of your own...

Love	Compassion	Honesty	Respect
Freedom	Passion	Intimacy	Happiness
Fun	Security	Health	Creativity
Contributing	Learning	Adventure	Caring
Adventure	Success	Excitement	Power
Independance	Personal Growth	Sharing	Winning

Now if you think about what you have chosen and how important these values are to you, then you will be able to imagine how living a life that enables you to express and experience these values would make you incredibly happy and passionate about your life.

What's missing for you?

When you have identified the most important values in your life, you can look at whether these values are being met, because if not, you now have a choice to do something about it. If creativity is something you value and therefore need in your life, allowing yourself to build into your life the things you truly value will give you back your passion and this in turn will help you feel fulfilled, happy, secure, expressed, etc.

Lighting the torch of passion!

Here is where the truth comes in; how are you going to live a life filled with passion and motivation if you ignore what you value most? The key is to find ways to live out the things you value the most and not deny they exist. Write down below how you can meet your values in your life, take the words you circled above and expand on them to give yourself an explanation of what you need in order to experience these values in your life, for example...

Love — to love and be loved.

Compassion — to express my compassion towards others.

Creativity — to be creative.

Adventure — to experience adventure.

Fun — to have fun in my life.

Respect — to respect myself and feel respected by others.

Health — to take responsibility for my health and to care for my body.

To help you understand what a 'value' is, try thinking of something you may value, for example 'being creative'; now imagine not being able to be creative ever again in your life, not being able to appreciate creativity in yourself, in others, in what you see and feel; imagine it just does not exist! If you feel like it would be an empty life, then this is something you value and simply MUST have in your life in order for you to feel complete!

?...

?...

?...

?...

?...

?...

?...

?...

?...

?...

?...

?...

?...

?...

?...

?...

?...

....

You can make your own list – all you have to do to increase
your passion is be TRUE to who you are.

"If you have the courage to begin – you have the courage to succeed.

Anon

Motivated by honesty

Once you're clear about your values and you feel the passion for the life you want, you can begin to set your goals, and your goals are simply to improve these areas of your life. The motivation to change your life for the better comes from the truth of who you really are and what you really want. In the chapter about goals you can take this truth and look at all the areas of your life and begin to set out your personal goals.

Being authentic

Can you remember a time when you made a decision in your life and it just felt right? If you can, then chances are you will understand that you were being real and authentic. This takes courage and comes from the heart; it feels instinctive and sometimes even spiritual. By learning to be authentic about who you are and how you may feel afraid to be yourself, you can release the truth of what you truly want and then you will be able to make decisions straight from the heart with passion and honesty.

This is not an easy thing to do, we set up all sorts of comfort zones, limiting beliefs and excuses to avoid facing these truths; but the reality is, the most successful people in life are the ones who face their fears and act from a place of authenticity, and this is where they feel a sense of freedom and release of passion for who they are.

What blocks motivation?

FEAR................blocks motivation. Be really honest with yourself here. What are you really afraid of? Who are you pretending to be? If you have identified who you really are and how you would like your life to be, then there must be a reason why you have not changed this before. Right? What is this reason?

To help you, here is an example of one person's life when he answered this question. To give you some background, he had come through a very painful and difficult divorce over a period of years and had lost his confidence.

He asked these questions and gave himself these answers:

Q Who would I like to be?

A. Attractive, happy, interesting and loved.

Q Who am I being/pretending to be?

A. Unattractive, unhappy, feeling stupid and unlovable.

Q How do I benefit from thinking like this?

A. I don't have to take responsibility; I don't have to risk being hurt again.

Q What is the price I'm paying?

A. I don't like myself or the way I look, my health suffers, my children have a parent with no confidence, I am alone, I am unhappy and I feel guilty for not being a better person – it's affecting everything.

So can you see what this person was doing? His self belief was very negative and this couldn't be changed until he looked at the truth of what he was doing to himself – he was being controlled by FEAR – fear that he was not good enough!

Are you feeling brave?

Go on then, try this for yourself! Write down honestly the answers to these questions and learn to take responsibility for what you think of yourself, so that you can make better decisions.

Who would I like to be?

....

Who am I being or pretending to be?

....

How do I benefit from thinking like this?

....

....

What is the price I have to pay?

....

....

....

....

Well done! That took courage, but you did it!

Create your dream board

Have some fun here and use your imagination to create a life that you would like to experience. This is where you can go wild and add things to your dream board that will inspire you and develop your motivation.

Take a big piece of paper or a clipboard and create a collage of images based on what you would like to experience. You could use images cut out of magazines, words, inspirational quotations, books of titles, photos of people you admire or who inspire you, places you want to visit, things you want to do, even down to the food you would like to eat! Remember to keep in mind the things that you value in life and whatever images/dream you come up with. Ask yourself: Is this really me? Do I really want this? Will it fulfil my values?

When you've finished doing your board, it should look bright and full of inspiration for you. Pin it up somewhere you can see it and use it to motivate you into action.

Patience and little steps

It is important to point out that it's human nature to want everything that makes us happy right now! However, look upon your dream board as a way to inspire you with your goals and then develop an action plan and take small steps forward, one thing at a time. (This is covered in the chapter on Personal goal setting.)

Building confidence fuels passion

A lot of confidence comes from our self-image, because how we think and feel about our own image affects our confidence. Today's society is extremely image conscious and it can often feel like a constant pressure from visual advertising on how we should appear and what success is meant to look like. This is one way we are reminded on a daily basis that we are not measuring up to the norm, but let's be realistic here, the norm is generated from big business marketing campaigns to get us buying as much as possible. So it's no wonder many of us are constantly unhappy with our self-image because we are trying to achieve the impossible, therefore we are always dissatisfied with what we look like.

The fact is that these perfect images of success are set unrealistically high for a reason – to keep us in a state of dissatisfaction with ourselves. We will never be able to attain them and therefore feel cheated and disheartened that whatever we achieve it never feels like enough, so we keep trying to achieve more and more in the hope that one day we will reflect what the advertisements tell us happiness is!

So that's my little rant and rave over, mainly because as a parent it is vital that we look after our inner confidence and not let the economic, social and public pressure dictate who we really are inside. Don't get me wrong though, improving your image and appearance and developing a strong and confident attitude and body posture, the way you behave and the way you speak to others, can make you look and feel more confident.

So let's start...

Focus on where you want to go – not on what you fear.

Anon

Be passionate about who you are

Confidence and a positive self image comes from feeling good about yourself and being comfortable with exactly who you are, so as much as you can, RESIST being pulled into the media models of image and success. Find a person who you identify with and make it someone that you admire for being truly themselves, look at how they express themselves and become more of who they are, rather than less.

Who do you admire?

Make a list of people you think are confident and express this, and then start to explore by writing down the things about yourself that you admire and like, for example you may be a great person to have as a friend, have artistic talents, enjoy singing, be good at your job, enjoy cooking, have nice hair, a lovely smile, whatever it is, think about how this is a positive element of who you are, allow yourself to like it about yourself and take credit for it.

Stop comparing

Now we all have people we admire and I must admit that some people are just beautiful and clever and so on and so on, however, it's a good idea to stop comparing yourself with others because whilst you are doing that you are not looking at your true self and admiring and developing the great qualities you have. Begin by admitting to yourself that there will always be someone more lovely, more clever, more interesting, more exciting etc. and that it is normal to want to be your best. The next step is to look at yourself as an original – a unique person in your own right. Take a few minutes now to think about whether you compare yourself to others and how this makes you feel; commit to stop doing this and realise that you are a very special person and there is only ONE of you in the whole world: you are totally unique. How amazing and priceless is that!

Act with confidence

There will always be times when we feel a bit negative about ourselves, this is natural, all sorts of things can influence our emotions and that's what makes us different and interesting. Being aware of how we feel is important, and taking some time to help ourselves is about taking responsibility for that.

The next time you feel negative about things, remember that it is a thought, a feeling and write that feeling down on a big enough piece of paper to stand on with both feet; then I want you to write down the feeling you do want to have on another sheet of paper. Place them both on the floor and stand on the negative one that you are experiencing at that moment. Stand on it for a few moments and allow yourself to think about why, what and how it is that you feel, take it all in and then when you are ready move off the paper onto the positive one, read it and think about it in your mind, imagine what that feeling feels like; perhaps you have gone from feeling angry and sad to happy and uplifted, so think about the positive feelings and imagine yourself experiencing them. Notice how you feel physically and lift your head up as you step off the paper. Now finally, take the sheet of paper with the negative feelings and rip it up into small pieces and bin it!

Wow! That feels good and every time you need a boost do this exercise and train your brain that it has a choice to think negatively or positively! If necessary get a big enough bin especially for the job!

Pressing the self-destruct button?

You know 90% of what we worry about never actually happens, and yet while we sit and think and worry about things we don't realise that our negativity is producing other negative experiences, and sometimes what we worry about can actually happen because we are so focused on this we lose sight of all the positive things.

I can give you a funny example of this; I remember baking a cake for my daughter's 5th birthday and it was a new recipe, so I wasn't sure how it was going to turn out; I was worried that it wouldn't rise in the oven and then the birthday party would be a disaster with no cake! As a result I checked on the oven at least three times, opening the door each time to see that it was baking properly – you know what happened! Of course it flopped in the oven because the cold air went in every time I opened the door! So you see, I created the one thing I was worrying about! My lack of confidence and fear actually created the very thing I did not want.

I have done this in so many other ways in my life, that I am now very aware when I start to worry about things that I have to be careful that I am not being self-destructive!

Take a moment now to think about whether you do this and commit to change this in yourself by **asking a different question** about your concerns or worries.

Questions you might like to ask yourself:

Q. If I worry about this, is it going to make any difference?

Q. Is there any action I can take that will make a positive difference?

Q. Can I decide to stop worrying about this? Yes or No.

Q. What is the benefit I receive from worry?

Q. If I worry about this – am I avoiding something else?

Be a completer

One of the fastest ways to give yourself confidence and a real boost to your self esteem is to complete what you started. Now that might sound obvious, but we all suffer from this and start off with the best intentions—such as New Year resolutions— with ideas and interests that feel exciting at the time, but then many don't get past the thinking about it part. Then there are all the half completed jobs that keep niggling in the back of your mind and the putting off becomes days, then weeks, then a month goes by and for some things, even years!

Make a list of all the things you wanted to do and started but have not finished, it could be sorting out a room at home, tidying your office, clearing the garage, decorating the lounge, writing that book or joining that club, whatever it was, decide if you still want or need to do it and why. If the reason is a good one, then make it a priority and take action on it today, allow yourself the pleasure and happiness of feeling really good that you finished something you said you were going to do and YOU DID!

Say what you mean!

Practise saying what you mean – not what you think people want to hear. Be yourself and listen to your internal voice that tells you what you would like to say. There are always times when it is wise to say nothing and to wait for a better moment, but on the whole, if you practise being clear about what you really want to say it can save a whole lot of worry and misunderstanding. Easy to say I know, but start to practise it with someone you would really like to be straight with, perhaps you know a person who is always judgemental of others or makes negative comments. Why not start with this person and commit to saying something positive or what you really mean the next time you see them.

For example, a relative or person makes an unnecessary comment; you could go along with it and join in, or imagine how liberating it would feel to say "Well actually I don't agree, I think ...." By doing this you are taking control of your life and this will give you confidence in other things. Often the people we find it the hardest to say what we mean to are those closest to us.

Write down a list of those people with whom you find it hard to say what you mean and next to the name write down what you would like to say to them.

Now take the easiest one on your list and commit to make a small step in the right direction by saying exactly what you mean the next time you see them. It doesn't have to be a big thing, but it does need to be what you would like to say and not what you think they want to hear! Go on, go for it – you know you want to!

Positive talk and feedback

I really like it when people are straightforward and say what they mean, even though I know it is sometimes hard to hear, especially if I'm asking a question and their answer throws me.

Of course there is a way of saying what you mean and this comes with confidence. I take the view that, if it is going to help someone to talk straight with them, then this is the best thing to do, even if it feels hard to do. Talk straight with yourself first and act with positivity.

Who needs to know?

Often giving feedback to others reflects our own fears or misunderstanding of another person; to be sure that the feedback we give or the need we have to tell another person how we feel is justified, try writing a letter to yourself first putting in all the things you want to say and why you need to say it, how you feel and how you feel it will help them. Read the letter through a couple of times and if possible with a day or two between writing it and reading it again. Now ask yourself who is going to benefit from the letter? Does the letter (or feedback) really need to be given or has writing it down had a positive effect and you have learnt something about yourself by doing it?

In my experience, there is no such thing as constructive criticism, it is criticism and words do stick in people's hearts and minds. Ask yourself – do your words build this person or knock them down? Then you will know what to do.

Summary

- Develop your passion by deciding what you love or dream of doing and being honest with who you are.

- Getting stuck in the 'comfort zone' will put out the light of passion and motivation.

- We are all born with natural enthusiasm and passion, motivation to be our best. Don't give up who you really are and always hold onto your dreams.

- If you know what you value, and then develop a life that fulfils those values, you will be living with passion.

- Create a dream board – collecting images, ideas and quotes in one place to inspire you.

- Self image affects confidence, so take pride in self image and this will develop a strong and confident attitude.

- Feel comfortable and passionate about who you are. Resist the pull of images of success – you are unique!

- Connect with someone you admire and look at the qualities this person has; write down how you could develop these positive elements inside yourself.

- 90% of what we worry about never actually happens and negativity produces self-destructive behaviour.

- Finish things off, it's a good feeling when you complete something you started.

- Practise saying what you mean and not what you think people want you to say. Be clear about what you mean.

Life changes the moment you make a decision to commit to developing yourself - to know oneself is to think for oneself!

Anon

Setting personal goals

chapter 4
Setting personal goals

Knowing exactly what you really want is a big question, but it's all important if you are going to create a happy and fulfilling life; but knowing why you want those things in your life is the key to moving forward and having the life you want. So in order to understand what motivates you it is essential that you know what you value and what is important to you, this is what makes you as a person and directs you to the things in life you want to feel and experience.
(See Chapter 3 – *Finding your passion*.)

A great place to start is by asking yourself some honest questions about how happy you are with all the different areas of your life. Often it is a lack of confidence what stops people feeling clear about what they want and setting their goals. Are you as confident as you would like to be? To feel confident in yourself you will need to feel confident that it is possible to succeed in what you really want and to believe that your ambitions, needs, and deepest desires really do matter!

So by working on this area of your life and being really honest with yourself about your life right now, it will help you to set goals to make positive changes and help you to see clearly what you really want; this will motivate you forward, then moving one step at a time to gain confidence from addressing the things you want to change or improve in your life.

Develop your strengths

Take a pen and write your name vertically down the page here and for each letter I want you to write something positive about yourself.

So for example my name is Simone and here are words I, or others, have said about me which are positive.

S   =   sensitive

I   =   interesting

M   =   motivating

O   =   optimistic

N   =   natural

E   =   enthusiastic

Just have a play with the words and remember they can be words to describe who you are or what you do, or even how you would like to be, as long as they are positive!

Now imagine having a go at listing your strengths and write down what makes you special and wonderful. Would you find this easy to do?

How about writing down a list of your weaknesses? Many people find it easier to list these than the positives; we are generally pretty hard on ourselves and the fact is, you may be hiding behind the fact that you are actually afraid of being positive and truly expressing your strengths. So what are your strengths exactly?

Create affirmations

Support what you feel about yourself with an affirmation. Give yourself some positive statements about yourself which are all in the present tense. For example, how about one of these or a mix of them; whatever you believe about yourself, even if you are not convinced – try it now!

I am attractive and intelligent.

I am good at my job.

I am a great person.

I am special and interesting.

I am ....

Whatever you decide, write down your affirmation here in the space provided and read it over and over and then say it to yourself each morning. Whatever you focus your attention on is what the brain is responding to. Remember it is easy to fill your brain with the worries and negative thoughts, so block them out and create a new positive thought process that is empowering for you!

Do you know what your goals are?

On the following two pages is a list of the most common life areas that people feel are important and of value to them, although they may not be exactly the same for everyone, it's a good place to start. Take a look at each area and think about how you feel about each one. This is just for you to see, so go on be really honest about it and don't miss anything out.

Scoring your life areas

Score the life areas below out of 10 for how happy and content you are with each one. 1 being a low score because you are very unhappy about it, 9 or 10 because it's just perfect and maybe a 5 or 6 for an area that needs improvement. Take a look at how the scores impact on each other, for example money is often related to work and home, whereas a low score on partner might have an impact on health and well-being, and particularly your emotional well-being!

Here are the 8 life areas:

1. Health and well-being

   How do you feel about your emotional, mental, physical and spiritual sense of well-being? How much positive energy do you feel?

   Score ....

2. Work and Career

   How is your work and do you have the career you want or are you working towards this area of your life? Are there any difficulties here?

   Score ....

3. Money

   This one is interesting – we often feel like we don't have enough, but be honest and ask yourself is this really the case? What do you really need to be happy?

   Score ....

4. **Family and Friends**

   How are your relationships here, do you have enough time for your family, parents, children? Is it quality time? Are there difficulties?

   Score ....

5. **Partner**

   Whether or not you have a partner or someone special to share your life with, the important thing is how you feel about it, honestly!

   Score ....

6. **Personal Development**

   Are you learning new things about yourself and others and developing as a human being? An example might be new motherhood, doing a training course, studying for a job, travelling or contributing to others.

   Score ....

7. **Fun and Leisure**

   Ah yes, do you get time for this? Do you make time for it? Do you do too much of it and not enough of other things that you know are important to you? This area is just as important as anything else.

   Score ....

8. **Environment or Home**

   Where you live, your neighbourhood, the home you live in and the people you live with or near to, all have an impact on how you feel.

   Score ....

"Always look at how far you have come – not how far you have to go.

Anon

Now look at your scores

Great, so now you have given them all a score and made some connections to areas that influence each other, you will be able to see both negative and positive connections, and what you may find interesting is that the area that is the highest score is the one area that you have no problem putting a lot of time and effort and energy into; you enjoy working on this area of your life because you value it very highly and you gain happiness and pleasure from making an effort in this area.

However, the scores that are lower may be the ones you have been avoiding because they feel painful or you find them difficult to address. The important thing to remember here is about working to achieve balance in all these areas of your life. As you will see, when one area is out of balance it will have a knock-on effect on the other areas of your life.

It is also important to point out that as we all strive to achieve a good balance in all these areas, sometimes things come along in life that we did not expect and throw great plans out of the window. However, you now know that you can do this exercise any time you feel things are out of balance and see exactly where the challenges are for you and how they are making you feel, so that you can address the balance and do something about it.

Score a goal!

The scores that are low become your goals. To improve those areas in your life, you can begin to be specific now and look at exactly what you would need to do to improve the scores by just one mark to start with!

First let's imagine that you don't do anything about these scores at all except just look at them and then close the book and move on. I want you to imagine now what your life will look like 12 months' time and having done nothing about any of the scores to improve them I want you to score them again; what will have happened if you just left everything as it is? And if that begins to look negative, I then want you to move forward in time another two years and imagine where you live, your work, family, health, relationship and having done nothing about those low scores now for three years, what does you life look like?

Taking action now

If you want to improve those scores then now you will begin to understand the force of what motivates you. Perhaps it is to change something to move away from it or to move towards something better; whichever it is, you will now begin to see how to find your motivation easily if you are honest enough with who you are and what will happen if you don't take responsibility yourself for what you want.

Taking action is crucial to moving forward and when you move forward you will automatically feel your confidence growing. As you become more and more true to yourself, you will be able to feel your inner confidence and inner strength develop.

Making a commitment!

Choose the area in your life that you feel is **the most important right now** and which you know will have the biggest impact on your life if you take steps to improve it. Choose one of these and write down your goal next to it:

Health and Well-being ....

Work and Career ....

Money ....

Partner ....

Personal Development ....

Fun and Leisure ....

Environment/Home ....

My goal is:

....

....

....

I am going to take the following action now to move one step closer to my goal and to become more true to myself:

....

....

....

....

I am going to take this action (when exactly?!):

....

....

....

....

I am committed to this first step, the only thing holding me back is:

....

....

....

....

....

I am going to overcome this by taking action on:

....

....

....

....

....

Now I am 100% committed to my goal and it starts NOW!

CONGRATULATIONS!

Summary

- Increase your chances of success in life by being a goal focused, forward looking and positive person.

- Looking at all the areas of your life and scoring them will highlight what is working and what is not; with this greater awareness you can begin to set goals to improve them.

- Moving one step at a time towards your goals will ensure you don't worry about failing.

- Giving yourself positive affirmations about your strengths will encourage motivation.

- When you see an area of your life working well, know that this is where you are putting in particular energy and effort.

- Looking at your life 12 months from now will help you to become aware of the impact that not working on your goals will have on your life.

- Take action to move forward with your goals and dreams and get into the habit of taking action on a daily basis.

- Taking a 'can do it' approach to anything that feels like a problem or challenge will keep you positive.

- People who write goals down are 80% more likely to achieve them than those who don't.

- If you don't take action to achieve the results you want in your life, then who will do it for you? Taking 100% responsibility for your life is the first goal to master.

Don't waste ill health – use it to heal your life!

Richard Wilkins

Well-being & life balance

chapter 5
Well-being & life balance

Well-being means our whole life where we are achieving a sense of balance in our health and the food we eat, our working lives and relationships, our fun and adventures and leisure time as well as our personal sense of achievement or sense of fulfilment.

It makes sense that having good health and a real sense of well-being will give us a better chance of achieving the life we want; no amount of money or wonderful material assets we gather in our lives will be worth anything to us if we don't have a mind and body to enjoy it all.

Well-being and lasting change

The words well-being are used all the time to describe and sell everything from the latest diets to face creams, food for our children, and endless marketing campaigns use it on television and the Internet in order to get us interested in their products. However, don't be put off by hearing these words all the time; to bring about lasting changes we need to decide which areas of our lives are going well and which ones need improving. Staying motivated and taking small steps with clear goals is a lot easier than taking huge leaps into the unknown.

(refer to Chapter 3: *Finding your passion* and Chapter 4: *Setting personal goals.*)

So how is your well-being today?

How do you feel now, do you have a sense of well-being? Is your life in balance? Using the selection of words others have used before to describe well-being, take a moment to circle the words below that you would use for yourself and add any others that you consider important!

Calm	Content	Fulfilled	Peaceful
Happy	Healthy	Fit	Energised
Spiritual	Sense of purpose	Control	Connected
Joyful	Grateful	Respected	Confident

Do you feel this in your life? Do you have that sense of life balance and well-being?

If you do then that's a great place to be and you can look at how to maintain that with your goals. If you don't have that feeling, then circle the ones you would like to feel and this can help you with your goal setting!

Visualise health and well-being

Learn how to improve your health and well-being and you will have a much better chance of creating the life you want. Take a moment to try this visualisation technique and imagine your body is a car...!

Imagine you were going on a round the world trip and needed to buy a car for the journey. Would you buy a car that had no air in the tyres or water and oil in the engine? Or a car that had not been serviced and was struggling to start? Would this car fill you with excitement and security about your long journey ahead? OK, so joking apart, imagine your body is the car, you expect it to get you through the journey of your life without letting you down, but do you look after it and make sure it is fit for the job? Most of us take our bodies for granted until something goes wrong. So it makes sense to look after our bodies and keep them healthy, which in turn will give us confidence to face life's ups and downs.

Make a commitment today to give your body what it needs. Start by giving yourself a reality check and this will also provide you with more motivation!

Ask yourself these questions and write down the answers
How do I rate my sense of well-being today out of 1-10?

Score .....

Give yourself an overall score and then ask yourself the questions below.

1. How long can my body cope with this?

   ....

2. What can I do to help myself?

   ....

3. What will happen if I don't bother?

   ....

4. When can I begin to do this?

   ....

"

The human body is
the best picture of
the human soul.

"

Ludwig Wittgenstein

Healthy pressure or unhealthy stress?

Do you understand the difference between pressure and stress? We live in a culture that is constantly focusing on stress, however it's important to remember that not all stress is bad! For example, sitting an exam, competing in a race or competition, going for a job interview or even getting married all create a certain level of pressure or stress. However, we know through research that this can be a positive pressure and even working under a certain amount of pressure is exciting and motivating, some people actually thrive on high levels of pressure. The problem comes when unhealthy amounts of pressure turn into feelings of stress, which if not dealt with will persist and take its toll on our health and overall well-being – then we begin to feel beaten up by the stress.

Managing stress

Learning how to manage the stresses you experience in life ensures you maintain your health and well-being, as stress (when it is stored up and not dealt with) will start to impact on your health. It's not always easy to recognise in yourself when you are suffering from too much pressure and you are becoming stressed. The first step to help yourself is to take a coaching perspective on what good health and well-being means to you, from this point you will begin to recognise the areas in your life that cause you to feel stressed and how the negative effects of stress are affecting you and your life. You are now able to set clear goals to ensure you beat stress before it beats you!

Know your body – your stress triggers

Knowing your body and how you behave under pressure is the first important step in taking control of negative stress. Here is a list of some of the behaviours that may be triggered in you when you start to show signs of feeling stressed. It's important to remember that everyone is different and what would make some people feel under pressure and stressful can be exciting for others. Think about a time when you felt under a lot of pressure in your life—it could be at work, school, home, family, relationships—and what were your stress triggers.

- Low on energy and always tired.

- Headaches and muscle tension.

- Not sleeping well and restless at night.

- Rushing everywhere all the time.

- Overeating or eating food you don't usually eat.

- Over drinking or having drinks you don't usually have.

- Feeling moody and snappy.

- Taking more exercise or ceasing to exercise.

- Feeling anxious and jumpy.

- Feeling overwhelmed and unfulfilled.

- Feeling emotional and tearful.

- Feeling forgetful and confused.

Can you relate to any of these feelings, behaviours and symptoms?

Write down here the things you recognise in yourself when you begin to feel stressed so you can use it as a way of reminding yourself to take notice and do something positive to help yourself feel better:

....
....
....
....
....
....

What I can do to take the pressure off

Write down here the things you have done in the past that have worked to help you feel more relaxed and in control, ask yourself when you last did this for yourself and how would it benefit you today to do this when you feel your stress triggers:

....
....
....
....
....
....
....

Positive psychology

Positive psychology provides a way forward in understanding who you are and how you feel about your life. Take a look at the following areas to see how your feelings of mental well-being associated with good work-life balance rate today. Psychologists suggest that there are a range of factors that provide a person's sense of well-being. Where are you on this list?

- You feel in control of your life (**control**).

- You feel healthy and well (**well-being**).

- You get enjoyment from your life (**enjoyment**).

- You have a sense of gratitude and thankfulness (**gratitude**).

- Work provides something other than money (**vocation**).

- You know what's important and you prioritise time for those things (**importance**).

- You feel connected, not isolated (**connection**).

- You feel good about yourself (**self-esteem**).

Give each one of these areas a score between 1 and 10 and this will help you to look more deeply at your life and where you could begin to change areas in order to improve your sense of well-being.

Make a decision to become healthy and invest your time now into how you can achieve this. Having good health and well-being is the key to your success in life and that has a direct effect on those you care about too. Do it for yourself and do it for them!

Boost your mental well-being

Which areas did you score high/low on?

Which areas need attention?

Where will improvements make the biggest difference to your life?

What do you need to work on? What are the priority areas for you?
What actions are you prepared to commit to in order to make improvements?
What can you do now and/or in the longer term?
Who could help? Where could you get support?
What do you do when you get stressed out?

Now make your own list here of the 4 main things you do when you feel stressed out:

1. ....

2. ....

3. ....

4. ....

Move away from negativity

Do people choose to stay unhappy or negative? We all know people who, no matter what is happening in their lives, always seem to focus on the doom and gloom! Even when things are looking up, they focus on being negative about themselves or negative about those around them or the world they live in.

The question is "Why?" Well, if you think about it, a person who is negative usually gets a lot of attention for their complaining and moaning and people get drawn into sympathising with them and constantly trying to reassure them that everything will be all right! Are you smiling now? Because you probably know someone like this and often feel like saying "Stop moaning and just get on with it". The problem is this person may well be stuck in his or her own negative comfort zone and why would they want to change, when they get so much attention?

Challenge the comfort zone!

Remember this, YOU have all the resources inside you to help yourself change things for the better, all you need to do is understand, acknowledge and then take responsibility for yourself in order to move forward again. Here is how you start!

Adopt a healthy lifestyle

If we eat a healthy diet, exercise regularly and ensure we get adequate rest our body is better able to cope with stress when it occurs. It's a fact!

Learn to say NO

Know when to say no and do not take on too much. We cause ourselves a great deal of stress because we do not like to say no to people. We like people to like us and don't like letting people down, so often we take on more than we should. Allow yourself to be assertive and learn to say NO without upsetting or offending people, start with small steps and make it part of a daily habit. If you feel stressed by having to say no then the chances are you don't want to say yes but you tell yourself "If I don't say yes I will feel guilty" – right? So don't feel guilty, change your behaviour and see what happens! Start today and learn to say what you mean!

Determine what causes you stress

Identify what causes you to become stressed and then try to change your behaviour to reduce it; again start with small steps – one thing at a time.

Avoid unnecessary conflict

Don't be too argumentative. Is it really worth the stress? Look for the win-win situations. Look for a solution to a dispute where both parties can achieve a positive outcome.

Manage your time more effectively

We waste a lot of time doing unimportant tasks. Prioritise your day and do the important jobs first. The unimportant ones can wait, and often they will disappear completely leaving you time to do other things. Also do not put off the unpleasant tasks; you can guarantee that every time you think about them you feel guilty and that causes negative feelings about yourself, causing unnecessary stress.

Recharge your batteries

You will perform in every area of your life much better after a break and easily make up the time you use relaxing. When you begin to feel stressed allow yourself a few minutes to switch off, go for a walk, make a cup of tea, but stop what you are doing and give yourself that much needed time to let the pressure off, you don't have to be superman or superwoman, just be yourself and be kind to that mind and body you own!

Why not pin a post-it-note on your PC or in the house, maybe on the bathroom mirror, where you will notice it and spell out "HAVE I TAKEN A BREAK TODAY?"

Creating energy and vitality

Coach the life and vitality into your life with The 8 step challenge. Try this for 8 days and see the results for yourself!

Step 1 - Breathing

Breathing in oxygen gently yet deeply at the start of each day will really energise you; it will only take a few minutes, but it is vital to start off your day in a positive mindset. Taking a few moments to yourself to breathe in and out deeply is about looking after yourself from the moment you wake and before you go into your day with all the demands it may take from you. It's a way of reminding yourself that you are important, that you want balance and to feel happy.

Simply stand in a space where you can lift your arms high and with your feet hip width apart, breath in deeply through your nose and gently lift your arms high above your head; count 1 as you raise your arms, hold the breath for a count of 4 and then lower your arms counting for 2 and breathing out – that's 1-4-2. Now repeat this 4 times and each time you repeat concentrate on your breath, keeping it gentle, easy and flowing. It is not a test or race, the idea is to focus your mind on yourself and your body for a few moments each day.

When you get into the routine of doing this, then you can do it for longer and at any time during the day when your energy is slowing down or you feel a little stressed; it's all about your taking control of how you feel. Of course practice in the fruit and vegetable aisle at the supermarket or your open plan office might bring a smile to a few faces!

Step 2 - Water

Water is a really easy one. Our bodies are made up of 70% water and when we don't have enough hydration, our body slows down, our internal systems that digest our food become sluggish and this can affect our mind, which in turn can effect our emotions; we can feel tired, get headaches and feel generally slower with no energy. All it takes is to keep an eye on how much water we take in. We tend to drink tea and coffee without thinking, but simply adding in a few glasses or handy bottles of water as you go about during the day, will lift your energy levels and give you a boost.

Step 3 - Exercise

There are so many types of exercise the list is endless, the important thing to remember is choose something you really enjoy and like doing, it could be dancing or swimming or cycling, whatever it is, you decide and make a commitment to start today.

I wanted to lose weight many years ago and set my goal to get fit and lose 4 stone in 1 year. I decided to take up running, but I wasn't fit enough to run and needed to start with little manageable steps. I bought myself some basic running shoes and went for a 1 mile walk to see how it felt; I was pleased that I'd made the first effort and done it, the next goal was another small step, this time to walk 1 mile twice a week and I managed that too.

After a month of keeping up my walking routine, I set my next small goal and began jogging a bit on the 1 mile walk and then a month later increased it to 3 times a week. I was really beginning to feel the difference and my energy levels and spirits were lifting; I noticed that I was becoming more toned and didn't get tired after my walks anymore and the jogging was slowly helping to shift the weight.

I did reach my end goal and step-by-step I finally became a runner and lost the weight as I combined exercising 3 times a week and eating a good balance of nutritional food. After 1 year I ran a half marathon, had lost 4 stone in weight and I felt amazing. I really did feel like a different person and I was so proud of myself.

Don't allow yourself to be put off by feeling overwhelmed by your life goals. The thing to remember is it takes lots and lots of small steps; when you break down the big goal into bite size steps you move forward little by little and you take away the fear of failing the big goal, because you move forward with your small goals staying on course to achieve the end result. So whatever your exercise goal, be gentle with yourself and start the journey – then go step by step!

(Please seek expert medical advice first if you have any concerns about your health or exercising.)

Step 4 - Food glorious food
Here's how to enjoy food and keep it healthy:

- Eat plenty of fruit and vegetables.
- Eat a balanced diet to ensure you get enough nutrition.
- Eat when you are relaxed – not on the go and rushing.
- Eat comfortable amounts.
- Eat organic as much as possible.
- Eat well before the time you retire.

Step 5 - Direct your mind

Use your mind to think positively about yourself and your life in order to create happy feelings instead of stress and negativity; think of solutions to problems and ask problem-solving questions; think about what you eat and how you live your life and take action to change old habits and patterns of behaviour.

Step 6 - Support yourself

Looking after yourself will support you in the 8 Step challenge.

Take some time to rest and if possible get some sunshine, have a massage or do something gentle and nurturing for yourself; what's more, it doesn't have to cost money to support yourself – getting enough sleep, enjoying a walk in the park or just sitting still and relaxing with the newspaper or your favourite magazine or book; you must give yourself time out!

Step 7 - Watch the fats and oils

Keep a diary of the fat and oil you use in the first few days of the challenge, or just reduce your intake of fat and oil by half, give yourself a budget of butter, oil or fat for the 8 days and make it last. Try mixing water and oil in a cooking sprayer – you can buy these in most cook shops and this will automatically reduce your fat and oil intake.

Step 8 - Hidden addictions

Foods and drinks containing high amounts of sugar, salt and vinegars can become addictive to the taste buds and too much of them may impact on your health. Cutting out these things for 8 days will enable you to see and taste the difference in your food and drinks, which will help you realise how good food tastes without all the high amounts of sugar, salt and vinegar!

Summary

- Well-being is about your whole life, mind, body and spirit as well as the physical element of feeling healthy and fit.

- If you have a good balance in all areas of your life it will increase your feeling of well-being.

- No amount of money or material assets will give you a perfect sense of well-being if you neglect areas like relationships and health.

- Your well-being is unique. Understand what that is and strive to achieve this each day.

- Visualise your good health and well-being; it will make it easier to achieve when you believe and see it is possible

- For positive change look honestly at your life. Your body and mind reflect how well you feel about it.

- Pressure and stress are a part of life. Learning to say No to things takes the pressure off when you really need to.

- Unhealthy amounts of pressure turn into stress and can take their toll on your health, happiness and success.

- Find ways to de-stress, whether it's a long walk, reading a book or time off from the PC.

- Identify your stress triggers and take action to relax before negative stress builds up

- Being around positive people will ensure you stay motivated and not stressed.

- Laughter is a great stress reliever!

A great place
to meet is on
equal terms.

Anon

Relationships & communication

chapter 6
Relationships & communication

Understanding ourselves is the key to understanding others; when we learn to be open and honest about ourselves then it allows others to do the same in return. A great relationship is one when we feel comfortable about being ourselves, feel most alive and that we are learning, developing and growing as a person, so it makes sense that the way we communicate with each other is an important element of understanding in all our relationships.

Good communication is at the heart of every successful relationship, it allows people to express themselves, educate others and inspire. There are no limits to the opportunities to practise and expand your communication skills. Being a good communicator is key to success in life and you don't have to be a speech maker; you are communicating even before you open your mouth or put pen to paper, so be aware of the signals you're sending out, as the way you look, your body language, and your words all have an impact.

First impressions count

We communicate to others with our body language and appearance so fast, that it takes less than 10 seconds for a person to get a first impression and make a judgement of who we are.

Assess your communication skills

Take a moment to look at how you currently communicate and this will create a better awareness for you and therefore help you to make better choices if you want to improve this area of your life.

Q. When other people are talking to you what are you most likely to do:

A. Give them my full attention and remain silent.

B. Listen and repeat back what they said.

C. Start thinking about my own things I need to do.

Q. How do you feel when you have to say no:

A. I find it one of the hardest things to do.

B. It usually takes me some thought to get it right.

C. I have no problem saying no and meaning it.

Q. When you have to confront someone about an important issue:

A. I get someone else to do it for me.

B. I do it face to face, but get someone to support me if necessary.

C. I do it and get the job over and done with.

Q. How do you feel about talking to large groups:

A. I find it very uncomfortable and don't want to do it.

B. I am happy to do, providing I feel prepared.

C. I love doing it and embrace the opportunity.

Mostly As

You're more of a listener than a talker and may lack a certain amount of confidence when it comes to speaking out for yourself. You see communication as important but not an essential tool for your own progress. Ask yourself if you would benefit from improving your communication and how your life would improve if you did; write down your thoughts here:

....
....
....
....

Mostly Bs

You understand that good communication is important and you try to prepare and plan so that you express yourself as clearly and effectively as possible. However, you may follow a style of communicating that is structured and if you haven't ticked any Cs at all, then it may be that you are a good mediator but hesitate to project your own message to others. Ask yourself if you would benefit from expressing what you feel is important to others and how this might have a positive impact on your life; write down your thoughts here:

....
....
....
....
....

Mostly Cs

You are confident and forthright and feel very much at ease with the idea of being yourself and expressing yourself clearly to others. However, true communication is a two-way exchange of ideas. Could your forthrightness be blocking out the opportunity for others to express themselves to you? Might you be ignoring those opportunities or be failing to seek the opinions and attitudes of others? You might want to encourage feedback from others to help you build their positive ideas and opinions into your own communication; it's all about a win-win opportunity.

Being a good listener

Are you a good listener? If you can't see how listening is going to help you express yourself to others, then you might need to listen more than others! Whether your goal is to get others to agree, make yourself heard, instruct or motivate others, then communication is the key, however, many problems occur from failure to communicate, leading to misunderstandings and then mistrust. This is usually caused by a failure to listen – a fundamental element of communication. If you want to influence people, you first need to know how they think, and good listening skills will help you to achieve what you want.

TOP TIP

Remember this when you want to communicate well…
We were given two ears and one mouth because listening is twice as hard as talking. Is it all about me?

Positive communication

1. Listen actively to others, stop what you are doing and concentrate on what they are saying.

2. Turn off your mobile phone!

3. Show the person you have made time to listen to them.

4. Face the person and turn your body towards them.

5. Maintain eye contact with them and nod your head if you agree.

6. Ask questions which show you are listening and want to know more.

7. Clarify and confirm any mixed messages you may be picking up.

8. State your opinions or views only when they have finished!

Negative communication

Don't:

- Allow your mind to get distracted or day dream – it will show!
- Interrupt people when they are talking.
- Jump in and finish their sentence.
- Look at the clock or your watch all the time.

Interrupting a person when they speak suggests you lack the time or the patience to hear someone out and this means you will never really hear what the person is saying to you, or worse that you don't think they are worth listening to!

Understand the impact of your negative or positive state of mind on your relationships. Do you live in fear and worry about things or are you positive and relaxed and comfortable in the right now? Try this out – next time you have a conversation with someone close to you, your partner, a friend, your child or your own parent, listen to the words you say and the way you speak to them. Catch yourself talking and what you are talking about, do most of your sentences start with 'I' or 'my' or do you ask 'how' 'when' or 'why' questions?

Often a person who is focused on themselves controls the conversation with their need to discuss everything relevant to them, their opinions and needs. If you met someone like that and had a conversation with them, would you enjoy that? Would you tell them how they sound? Probably not – the point is, try to recognise how you behave and it will shine light on the way you could improve your relationships.

Speak to people

It might sound really obvious, but there is nothing as pleasant as a cheerful word of greeting, whether it be to the postman or to a grumpy teenager who is at the 'grunt only' phase of life. You know the saying: "I used to wake up grumpy, but now I let him (or her) sleep in!"

Eating and talking at the same time?

Don't forget to stop and chat over food! Eating at the computer or whilst watching television prevents the opportunity to communicate, even if it's just the usual day to day stuff. People like to be heard and share.

Smiling is free

Smiling takes 14 muscles and yet it takes 72 to frown, so how about smiling at the stressed mum with a crying child in the supermarket? Make a point of smiling at people and see the response you get, it will lift your spirits and help you practise a positive attitude. By the way – don't let the really grumpy faces who refuse to smile back put you off, there is always someone very happy to receive a smile.

Smiling

Smiling is infectious
You catch it like the flu,
When someone smiled at me today
I started smiling too.
I passed around the corner
And someone saw me grin,
When he smiled I realised
I'd passed it on to him.
I thought about the smile
And realised its worth
A single smile like mine
Could travel round the earth.
If you feel a smile begin
Don't leave it undetected
Let's start an epidemic quick
and get the world infected.

"If you do what you've always done, you will always get what you have always got.

Anon

Medicine for the soul

Did you know that people who are depressed or ill can feel better and recover more quickly by laughing and smiling? A smile releases serotonin, a powerful neurotransmitter that makes us feel better.

What's in a name?

It's like music to a person's ears when they hear the sound of their own name and it shows that you are making a conscious effort to be interested. It's the simplest way of being meaningful to another person, so make a point of saying their name back to them in conversation, it will help them to feel more comfortable with you and more positive towards you.

TOP TIP
As the saying goes "If you don't have anything positive to say - then say nothing at all!"

Be generous with praise

Great communication in any relationship is based on trust and a few ill-chosen words that are critical of a person can be devastating to any relationship. However, someone who is known for being encouraging is always popular. So if you are not generally the type of person who gives praise to others, start to do it in little ways where you can and you will notice not just a difference in the way people see you and think of you, but it feels good to know you are helping others with encouragement rather than negativity.

3 sides to any controversy

Your side, the other person's, and the right one!
There are some battles that are just not worth undertaking, and others that are just not worth winning – even if you are right. Think about the long-term effect and the amount of energy it takes to battle over something negative. Ask yourself first if it will be worth all that effort and what will be the reward to you. If the reality shows that you don't actually win anything other than you confirming to yourself that you can win arguments, then is it really worth the point – or would your time be better spent concentrating on your happiness and goals?!

Sorry seems to be the hardest word…
"I'm sorry" may at times feel like the hardest words to say to someone – but they are THE most powerful. It might feel like you are being strong and sticking to your principles or opinions by not saying sorry, but when you say those words and mean it, you are released from negativity and empowered with positive emotions. Try it next time you don't feel like saying sorry and feel how it releases feelings of fear, anxiety and worry. Like anything in life, the more you practise the better you get.

A sense of humour
Some people are just naturally gifted with a sense of humour that makes other people laugh and it helps put people at ease. For you to develop your own sense of humour, look at the things about yourself that make you smile. Learn to allow yourself the opportunity of not always being perfect, take the pressure off and have a giggle at the things that didn't always go right, look at the other side of the situation and find something funny in it. This will help you to relax about yourself.

Speaking with confidence

Develop your confidence to communicate in work and relationships by joining a local public speaking club. They offer a supportive environment in which you can build up your public speaking and leadership skills. These clubs are friendly and help you in the art of speaking, listening, and thinking on your feet, skills that will enhance your self-confidence and personal growth, not just for work, but in all your relationships, helping you to become more assertive in a non-threatening environment.

Body language speaks volumes

Did you know a person makes a decision about another person within just moments of looking at them? Even before they speak, their opinion has been formed. That's because we all read each other through our facial expressions and body language as well as the voice.

In order to communicate well in all relationships it is said that you must first be aware of your emotions and learn how to control those emotions, because other people will be reading these emotions and making a judgement.

Assessing the emotions of others

If you are intimidated, angry, afraid or resentful your ability to communicate and motivate others will be limited. Being aware of how you feel and taking responsibility for those feelings is the first step and then you will realise how you are affecting others. Think about what you want to achieve and imagine how you will achieve this by feeling negative towards that person;

now imagine being calm and positive to help you communicate clearly and ask yourself which way is really going to get your message across and achieve the result you want.

Negative body language

Do you do any of these things when you feel angry, resentful, afraid? How would you feel if someone was doing them to you?

- Avoiding eye contact/looking downwards.
- Turning towards the door to go.
- Checking the time frequently.
- Folding arms across the chest.
- Scratching the back of the neck.

Be aware of how your body is communicating and by changing your body language, you will begin to feel differently inside about your emotions, you will be more aware and in control.

Building rapport

Building rapport with another person is part of great communication. When you are in good rapport with someone, you may have the same sense of humour, like the same things and feel connected from the start. It's a great feeling and yet it happens on a subconscious level. Actually what you are doing is subconsciously recognising that you like this person and what they are saying interests you, without realising you will automatically begin to mirror their behaviour in a similar way. If you were to look at yourself in rapport with another person, it would look like one person in a mirror reflecting back the same gestures.

A great way to observe this is in a restaurant. Look at the couples around you and the ones who look interested and attracted to each other will be in rapport. Watch their body language, the way they sit, how they cross their legs and their gestures which will imitate each other's without them knowing they are doing it.

Facing up to friction

Dealing with friction in relationships, wherever they are, either at home or at work will enable you to live with more peace and happiness, create positive energy and help you gain in confidence to be yourself. There will always be difficult people in life but good communication can go a long way towards removing negativity and misunderstandings.

Learn to face the friction in order to prevent it from escalating. It's vital to acknowledge a problem exists, otherwise it becomes internalised and we can become angry and frustrated, letting off steam with friends and partners.

Four minute fix

If someone is annoying you and you want to avoid a confrontation – try this:

- Ask yourself whether this person is reacting to you because they perceived something negative coming from you.
- Suggest to this person that you may have done something to upset them. Or have you rubbed them up the wrong way without knowing?
- Encourage them to point out exactly what their problem is with you.

- Listen to what they say and repeat their point back to them for clarity.

This will only take a few minutes, but from this point you will both feel better understood and be able to make a more positive decision about how to feel about each other; go on be brave and give it a try – it works!

Sharing feelings

It's easy to bluntly tell a person what you think, what you want or need them to do, however, it can lead to that person feeling defensive and responding negatively to you. How you phrase your words will affect the response you receive to what you have said.

- Think about what you want to express and state the facts.
- Think about how you feel about this.
- Consider what is causing you to feel like this.
- Think about the outcome you want.

Practise here with a situation you want to address:

For example

- Talking to my partner about money issues.
- Talking to my teenager about behaviour issues.
- Talking to my boss about a problem at work.
- Talking to my parent about health concerns.

There could be any number of things you really need to sort out and so far have not done – right! OK so do this exercise and come out with a plan of how you will tackle it in a positive way.

What is it that you need to express? Just the facts –
write them down:

....

....

....

....

....

....

....

How do you feel about this? For example, worried, angry,
unhappy etc . How is this affecting you? For example, not
sleeping depleted energy levels, tiredness? Write them down:

....

....

....

....

....

....

....

....

....

Think about the kind of positive outcome you want for both yourself and the other person. Write it down:

....
....
....
....
....
....
....
....

Think about what will happen if you don't express yourself. What will happen a week from now, a month or a year from now? Is that what you really want? Write it down so that it becomes a motivation for change and action:

....
....
....
....
....
....
....
....

Decide when and where is the best place to talk and make a commitment to get it sorted out and focus on your solution and positive outcome. What action are you going to take?
Write it down.

………………………………………………………………………………………
………………………………………………………………………………………
………………………………………………………………………………………
………………………………………………………………………………………
………………………………………………………………………………………
………………………………………………………………………………………
………………………………………………………………………………………
………………………………………………………………………………………
………………………………………………………………………………………
………………………………………………………………………………………
………………………………………………………………………………………
………………………………………………………………………………………
………………………………………………………………………………………

Now you have a constructive plan to help you discuss what you want and if necessary take it with you when you have your conversation, it will help you stay on track to explain all the elements of what you think and it will also show the person how serious you are about wanting them to understand what you think, feel and need.

Creating a brilliant relationship

Take some time to write down a list of the things you must have in a partner to feel happy and then circle the ones that are an absolute priority and a MUST HAVE and then look at the ones you would like, but could live without or make a compromise on. List what you do not want too! Doing this will help you to be clear about what you want and it will allow you to be honest with yourself. It will enable you to communicate these important elements from the start of any relationship.

Being honest about what you need and then being able to recognise that these needs are not being met earlier rather than later in any relationship, will help you make better decisions rather than hoping that things will change on their own. You can take responsibility for creating a brilliant relationship through talking about what you really need.

How to know what you need

Start with looking at what you value, what is important to you as an individual and you can use the chapter on 'Finding your passion' to clarify what you value and who you are. From this point you will be able to imagine a relationship with someone who has the same values! Look back over your past relationships and look at the values you both shared, were there conflicts around areas where you both took a different perspective? If you are in a relationship that might have conflicts, work out what you both need and whether these needs are being met, and look at whether it will be possible to achieve.

Summary

- Understanding yourself is the most important way of understanding others.

- Being in a great relationship will make you feel that being yourself is the best thing for the other person.

- Feeling comfortable with another person and being able to express yourself and how you feel is the key.

- Tone of voice, the words used, and body language all impact on communication.

- Learning to be a great listener is a fantastic skill to help you improve communication and understand yourself better.

- Preparing what you want to say will give you confidence and focus on expressing key issues.

- Maintaining good eye contact and nodding your head in agreement is a clear way of showing interest and understanding of what is being communicated to you.

- If you feel the need to finish other people'ssentences, reflect on why. Is it a positive way of communicating or does it disempower the other person?

- Using 'I' a lot in conversation shows an inability to listen. 'You' and 'we' is more respectful and positive.

- Smiling and just saying "Hello" is the easiest and most wonderful way to cheer up someone, and it has an amazing way of spreading a good feeling to others.

Finish each day and be done with it. You have done what you could. Some blunders and absurdities no doubt crept in; forget them as soon as you can. Tomorrow is a new day; begin it well and serenely and with too high a spirit to be encumbered with your old nonsense.

Ralph Waldo Emerson

Work & money

chapter 7
Work & money

Although work and money are connected, they also stand alone as important elements of everyone's life. How you decide to live your life is based heavily around the sort of work you do or would like to do, being happy in your work is one thing, however, being in control of your money is another. If you don't feel you are in control of this area in your life it can spoil all the hard work and energy you put into the things you value. For example, being in debt or having money worries can cause stress, which can affect your health, your relationships, your confidence and judgement. So it makes sense to get to grips with your money situation and also to look at how you can improve your work life.

Taking small, yet manageable steps to achieve your work and money goals will help you develop your confidence and empower you to live the life you want. The first step is to assess where you are financially and even if it appears negative, at this point you can start to create the solutions to improve your situation. Awareness is the key.

So whether having a lot or just a little money is important to you individually, having awareness and taking control of your work life and your finances is a vital part of feeling happy in your life, after all most of us spend most of our lives working so it makes sense to get it right. Money may give us more choices, but if you don't have a clear picture of what your financial situation is, then how can you feel confident about any decisions or choices you may want to take in life, because you won't know where you will end up.

Working for different reasons

People work for different reasons, what are your reasons?
Let's explore in more detail and set goals to improve this area of your life.

1. To meet other people and have company.

2. To earn money, which gives more choices.

3. To experience a sense of fulfilment.

4. To have a level of status and significance.

5. To make a difference and have a sense of vocation.

6. To keep busy and occupied.

Why do you work? It could be one answer or a combination of reasons.

Write down your answer here: .

....

....

....

....

....

....

Complementing who you are

Finding the right career is all about finding something that complements your natural strengths and allows you to develop and explore yourself in a way that suits you. Take a moment to think about the ideas you had when you first thought about what sort of job you would like to do, and remember what made you feel excited and filled you with enthusiasm. These feelings are fuelled by your inner self, the way you see the world, what you value and how you would like to experience life, so it stands to reason that finding a job or career that allows you to be who you are will make you feel happy and help you develop your strengths as that person.

The right or wrong job for me

What if your job not only paid the bills, but also made you happier and more successful? Well, now it can as long as you know what the right job for you really is. Don't feel pushed into doing any job in order to make enough money to pay the bills, take some time or get some expert advice to help you find a job that will enhance your life beyond money. Taking the time to do this will help you stay true to who you are and what makes you happy as a person, by understanding what you value, you will be able to know which direction to go in when it comes to finding a career or job. (Refer to chapter 3: *Finding my passion.*)

My ideal job is?

Do you feel deeply that your work is right for you?
Answer **Yes** or **No**.

Do you feel frustrated or irritated with an aspect of your work?
Answer **Yes** or **No**.

So do your answers make you question what you are doing currently in your job? What would you ideally like to do? Imagine your ideal job now and here are some questions to help you think it through. Write down your thoughts next to each one.

What would the job entail?

....

....

....

....

....

Is the job full time or part time and why?

....

....

....

How much money would you want to earn?

....

....

Where would you work, outside, inside office, at home?

……………………………………………………………………………………

……………………………………………………………………………………

What qualifications, training, and experience would you need?

……………………………………………………………………………………

……………………………………………………………………………………

……………………………………………………………………………………

Would you want to work for yourself or for others?

……………………………………………………………………………………

……………………………………………………………………………………

How far away from home would you work?

……………………………………………………………………………………

……………………………………………………………………………………

Would you need or want to move or live abroad?

……………………………………………………………………………………

……………………………………………………………………………………

……………………………………………………………………………………

Would you want to manage other people?

……………………………………………………………………………………

……………………………………………………………………………………

……………………………………………………………………………………

Great, now you have designed your ideal job, so take a look at your job description and ask yourself "If I saw this job advertised, what would I need to do in order to consider sending off my CV and applying for this role/job?" or "If I was creating this as a job or business for myself do I have everything in place to do this?" Which areas of myself do I need to improve for it to become a reality? Do I need new skills, develop my character/attitude, qualifications and do I need specific experience? From this point you have a goal and you can start to take the first steps to moving forward towards your ideal job.

What are you going to do first? It may be talk to someone, do some research or get more information on your ideas – write it here:

....

....

....

....

Where would I like to be in 5 years' time?

This is one of those questions that gets you thinking. Where you would like to be and where you are now may be two different places, but without having your goals clear in your mind, then you will be open to all sorts of influences and may end up in exactly the same position in 5 years' time. So have a plan of what you would like to achieve and how your life will look in 5 years' time; don't forget to look at all the things you value and the areas of your life and make sure they are included (refer to chapter 3 *Finding your passion* and chapter 4 *Setting personal goals*). This will help you when it comes to deciding on where you want to work, what you want to do, who you want to work with and how you could achieve it. By being honest with yourself first, then you can start to move closer to your work and money goals.

Don't be put off by change

One of the easiest ways of giving up on your hopes and dreams of an ideal job or career is FEAR! Don't be put you off with the thoughts of having to make changes to your life. It is important to take responsibility for any changes you make and take into consideration how it may effect other people, however, you have one life and it can sometimes feel easier to give into what others may need, rather than what you need in order to be yourself. Think it through, be sensitive to others, but don't talk yourself out of being your best, you have one life – make it a happy one!

Giving yourself rewards

Allow yourself the time and opportunity to appreciate how hard you have worked and what you have achieved in your life already. Sometimes it's all too easy to be in such a rush to progress and improve oneself, that you don't stop to look at how well you are doing and how far you have come. Look back through your diary over the past year or years and taking a coloured pen, mark all the dates that you felt you achieved something positive, had a great experience or did something positive for your life.

Think about your family, your job, your friends, things you changed for the better, things you achieved which have helped you in some way. Mark them all, because they are all positive, and reward yourself with something nice to remind you of how well you are doing. Whatever it may be, it's about you letting yourself deserve the reward and feeling good about your personal successes; they will motivate and inspire you to keep progressing.

Time management

Taking the 'time' to look at how you use your 'time' will help you to work and live more efficiently, allowing you more free time to relax and re-energise and do all the other things you enjoy apart from earning money and working.

Take a look at your typical working week, it doesn't matter what you do, if you go to work, if you look after your family, if you have retired, the point is to use your time to get the most out of your life.

Break down the week into the seven days and write a list of the things that you have to do, and the time it takes out of your week, then write in the things you would like to do and the things that you could fit in after that.

Now take a look at this week. If it doesn't change are you going to be happy with it and will it be a positive way of living your life? Do you have enough time for all the things you know are important to you or do you have too much time and need to be constructive? The main thing to recognise with this exercise is how you feel about the way you currently manage your time and then once you have this awareness, take responsibility to make small steps—one thing at a time—to allow enough time for all of your needs to be met.

Take one area that stands out for you as important because you have not allowed enough time for yourself to enjoy it and think of one thing you could change to manage time for this more effectively.

For example… Family, Friends, Partner, Home, Fun, Social Life, Health, Personal Development, and …Work and Money!

Today I am going to change this area of my life by doing one thing to improve my time management – this will be:

....

....

....

....

....

Feeling under pressure from work?

Make an appointment with yourself in your own diary to devote at least one or two hours a week to relax by doing an activity that you really enjoy, such as a long walk, a cycle ride, a swim, a massage, reading a great book or a visit to the gym; book it in to your schedule otherwise weeks will go by and although you really wanted to, you never found the time!

Sleep is wonderful

Make getting enough sleep a priority. If you are under extra pressure from work, then getting some early nights will reduce the experience. If you can't sleep, then reflect and write down your successes that day, no matter how small, even a friendly smile to a colleague; realise that being tired will make things seem 100% worse than they are and the pressure could turn into stress!

Last thing at night...

When you have things on your mind about work and you find it hard to get to sleep as all the questions are whizzing around in your head, keep a little notebook and pen on your bedside table and write down your thoughts; this helps to empty your brain onto paper allowing it to feel more relaxed.

Be kind to yourself

Be gentle with yourself, do things you love as often as possible and don't feel guilty. Tell that negative voice in the back of your mind that you do deserve some time out for yourself, otherwise chances are no one else is going to know how much you need it and before you know it weeks, months and even years have gone by and you feel like your life is mainly about work!

Laughing is a tonic

There are days at work and in life, when nothing seems to go right, it just happens sometimes, that's life. However, rather than letting it get you down, try giving yourself a tonic of smiling! To smile and laugh as much as you can will release happy hormones around your body and lift your mood. If you can't do that at work, then try a funny movie to make you giggle and chuckle and get into a positive state of mind. Once you've found something that just makes you giggle because it's so silly, then watch it over again whenever you need to get back to feeling positive, it works!

Take that break

Take at least a ten-minute break each day to ease off from your schedule. You can do this by taking a stroll, coffee break or by doing something equally relaxing. It can be so easy to stay at your computer or work through a lunch break, deadlines to meet and you want to give a good impression. However, no one will stop you from doing this to yourself and when you end up tired and unhappy in your job, feeling overwhelmed and under pressure, who will you blame? You can say NO; you can stop and you can look after yourself.

Stay on course

Having goals and taking responsibility is important, however, don't take yourself or life so seriously that it becomes stressful and you feel compelled to be perfect; realise that if you fail at something, it is not the end of the world, smile and know that you and your goals are important and you will dust yourself down and get back on track, and remember there is no such thing as failure – only delayed results!

Who do you spend your time with?

Remember that who you spend your time with is very important, as the saying goes "who you spend time with is who you become", so take a good look around and ask yourself honestly whether you really like the company you keep and do you feel positive being around these people, do you like being around them? For some people it's easy to get into the habit of being critical and negative; keep your distance from negativity, and those people who like to gossip as it can easily pull you in and you may end up feeling drained of energy. Look at how you could be positive in this situation or simply stay away from it. Take action and do one thing that will bring you closer to feeling happier today.

Head in the sand syndrome

Don't bury your head in the sand over money worries or debts, it can help in the short term to ignore something so important, however, eventually it will catch you up and then you will have so much sorting out you will wish you had taken control over it sooner.

So many people feel guilty for not understanding their finances or for getting into financial difficulty, whether it was deliberate or a mistake. One way to move forward and feel happy and free of anxiety is to get someone who can be objective and unemotional to help you FACE IT. It may feel uncomfortable to start with, even embarrassing, but so what, from this point you will be in charge and be able to make better decisions. Remember, whose life is it we are talking about here?

Is it your life or has money got all the control? You decide, but remember the longer you ignore it, the less control you have and more work you will have to do to put it right!

Saving money by working at home

It can sometimes be quicker to increase your income by saving some income! How about saving some money by working from home? More and more jobs can be done at home, so look at what you do and see if there is any time you could spend at home doing a job or an element of your existing job, for example emailing, making calls, working on your personal computer with the Internet. Could you spend one day working at home? This could save you money on travel, running car costs and stress, whilst giving you more flexibility for other life commitments such as family. Work out how much this would save you over a year and it will add up!

Budgeting money

It will help you to achieve your life goals if you know how much money you really need to live on and how much money you want in order to achieve your hopes and dreams. However, if you spend everything you have each month and don't budget for what you need as your life develops (for example a growing family, moving house, health, new experiences) then it is tempting to borrow money to maintain the lifestyle you want and have the finances to develop your life. That is understandable, however, having a budget that you can monitor will help you to avoid getting into debt and over stretching yourself financially; it will help you to look at what you really need and what you would like and be able to make plans to save money for things rather than borrow, because after all, borrowing is not like the friendly neighbour asking "Can I borrow your lawnmower – mine's broken down?" which is a free gesture; borrowing money involves paying it back—with the interest, which keeps adding up—and 9 times out of 10 you realise it would have been much, much cheaper to save and pay for it in cash!

Time to get it sorted

How much time do you have left in your life to organise your life and sort out areas of your life that need improving? If it's having the job or career you really want or making enough money for the things you would like, then here's a quick and effective way of looking at how much time you have to achieve it!

Work – Money – Life – how much time do I really have?

Take your present age and subtract if from 80 (which is an average age – if you are 80 already or think you will live to a longer age then choose a greater number).
Now multiply it by 12 for example 42, 80 - 42 = 38 x 12 = 456.

This is the number of months you're likely to have left in this life!

How quickly the months go by, so don't delay – start living today!

Summary

- Getting to grips with your finances will help you to set goals around work and life.

- Finding work that complements your natural strengths will increase your chances of being happy.

- If you feel frustrated about your job, then write down how to use your strengths, skills and abilities to change.

- When choosing work, first ask yourself what you would really like to do and then find a way to achieve this.

- Research all possible jobs, particularly on the Internet. An ideal job may turn up that you had not considered.

- Where you would like to be in 5 years' time? Write down how work and money fit in with your plans.

- Goals to increase your income or change your job can all be put off by 'fear'. Take 100% responsibility for the results.

- Stay motivated at work. Look back through your diary and highlight all your positive achievements.

- Manage your time and allow yourself a balance of work and time for the other areas of your life.

- A budget for your money will help you to stay in control of your life and increase your confidence and self worth.

- Make an appointment with yourself in your own diary for at least two hours a week that is just for you.

- Save money by working at home. Lower travel costs and stress from traffic, relax you and make you more productive.

Happiness is not
achieved by the
conscious pursuit
of happiness;
it is generally the
by-product of
other activities.

Aldous Huxley

Making a difference

chapter 8
Making a difference

You have taken the time to pick up this book and look at your life and how you could improve it, whether you are looking for motivation, clarity or progress, it is all centred around you! However, this chapter takes you one step closer to finding ways to develop a way of living that naturally causes you to feel happy daily and better still, it will invite you to generate happiness in your life from the heart.

Once you understand who you are and what is important to you by using the tips in the other chapters, you will then be able to consider an important element of living, which is contribution! Making a difference to the life you live in and the one you will leave behind is something we all think about and when you feel this, it gives a person a deep sense of purpose and in return peace, contentment and happiness.

We are all messed up and imperfect – thank God!

Who are you? What do you want? Where are you going in life? All these questions have been asked in the previous chapters, however, remember your imperfections are what make you unique! Everything you decide to do in your life starts and lasts with one simple intention; to make yourself happy and to make other people happy; on the way we all mess up and get it wrong, so give yourself a break. It is understanding all elements of who you are that will help you to see the way forward and know your purpose.

I want to make a difference

We often feel at a loss as to how we can have a positive impact on the world and the people around us. However, feeling helpless can often lead to us feeling useless and unable to know what to do for the best, we question our ability and then give in to negativity too easily. It is possible to enrich and rejuvenate your life with purpose, however, it is important to get rid of the word apathy and replace it with action. Too much time is spent thinking about what we could do or might do – if only we had more time, if only we had more money, if only we had more energy. So it has to start with ACTION.

Appreciating what you already have!

Firstly, it's good to start with a basic way of looking at the things you have in your life, as all too often we tend to take them for granted. To discover your purpose in life, you need to start with what you have already achieved! It can be too easy to focus on what you haven't got and constantly strive to achieve more and more without taking the time to look at what you already have!

Try taking a reality check and remember something that you are grateful for; remember something that you value in your life right now and how you have worked hard to achieve it.

Ask yourself these following basic questions

1. Does **anyone** love me?   Yes - No
2. Do I have **somewhere** to live?   Yes - No
3. Do I have **enough** to eat?   Yes - No
4. Do I have **interests** or hobbies I enjoy?   Yes - No
5. Am I **able** to earn a living?   Yes - No
6. Am I able to **look after** myself?   Yes - No
7. Is my **health** reasonably good?   Yes - No

If you get stressed about getting more out of life, then come back to these basics when that happens and remind yourself of what you do have and how valuable that is to you.

Don't sacrifice your humanity

Having affluence and achievement is all well and good, but if you lose sight of appreciating the good things you already have in life, you may well end up less happy with the more you achieve.

How many times do you hear successful people saying "If I had the time to do it all again, I would have taken the time to appreciate my partner, my children, my health, my parents" and so on.

If you were to think forward in time and imagine your life exactly as it is now—it has just moved forward in time 10 years—would there be anything that you might regret and feel you didn't appreciate along the way? Write it down here to help you appreciate the here and now.

I have lived on another 10 years and when I look back I wish I'd

....

....

....

....

....

....

....

....

....

....

....

....

Learning from our mistakes

Don't be afraid to make mistakes. There is an old saying that
people who haven't made mistakes haven't made anything.
Allow yourself off the hook here, you know we all make
mistakes and the point is to learn and develop positively from
them. Ask yourself today, I'm I holding onto old mistakes
that make me feel bad about myself and if so is this going to
prevent me from having the life I would like and a sense of
purpose that I would really like to feel? If you have, then dump
it in the bin now; it does not serve you any purpose and is
spoiling your future happiness.

Challenge your negativity

Be aware of any negative thoughts you might be holding about yourself and don't accept them! Challenge them; are they REALLY true, if so what is the evidence? Are you giving yourself a hard time and being highly critical of yourself? When you hear yourself sounding negative, tell yourself to cut it out and be gentle on yourself—tell yourself a positive truth—remember something nice and positive about yourself, something you do that pleases you or that makes others happy, then tell yourself out loud what that is.

Write down a list of things here that you can say to yourself when you feel negativity creeping in.

For example...
Think back to a time you felt really pleased with yourself and had a personal success, take a few moments to allow yourself to remember how it felt and bring those positive feelings back into your mind.

Write those positive feelings down here:

....

....

....

....

....

....

Stop blaming and start living

The moment you look at who you are and what you want, it can be easy to ignore the elements of your character that you are not entirely comfortable with! If we were are all totally honest with ourselves, then all sorts of imperfections would come to mind which we could pretend we don't have; after all it can feel uncomfortable to admit that we sometimes get it wrong or that we are not always a good or nice person. Take a moment to consider being straight with yourself about elements of your personality that exist and accept that is who you are sometimes. Stop blaming others for how you feel, when you may have had an influence on these areas of your life, and begin to take responsibility for all elements of who you are, the good the bad and the ugly!!

It is from this point of truth that you can begin to really start living and being yourself.

In need of a little inspiration

Ever see a movie or hear a story of someone who had courage or achieved great things with their life? Maybe a rags-to-riches story or an amazing sporting achievement that stands out because the person overcame enormous physical or emotional obstacles in their desire to succeed. Take up reading some good uplifting books, there are excellent biographies and great self-help books that keep your mind motivated and inspired to stay positive.

Discovering your purpose

When did you last experience happiness and gratitude?

The chances are it was when another person did something special for you, helped you out, gave you love or showed you that you are important in this world. It's natural to want and need this, that's what makes our lives so amazing; we have the ability to create so much happiness in the lives of other people with a really simple concept – love.

So it makes sense that in order to discover your purpose in life, you will realise this when you find the ability to be yourself and show the world who you are, and by loving yourself you will be able to give to and love others.

So here's the question – what opportunities do you have to show the world your love towards others?

Here are some examples to get you thinking:

- Being a loving parent, partner, friend, son, or daughter.
- Giving your time to others.
- Being a kind and caring person.
- Showing compassion to those less fortunate.
- Helping others without wanting in return.
- Looking after yourself, being responsible.
- Having respect and tolerance.
- Developing yourself to be your best.
- Inspiring others to be their best.
- Being encouraging and supportive.
- Being forgiving and understanding.

It also stands to reason that you can do these things when you are able to do this for yourself. So...

- Be loving towards yourself.
- Give time to yourself.
- Be kind to yourself.
- Show compassion to yourself.
- Give help to yourself.
- Take responsibility for yourself.
- Respect yourself.
- Be tolerant with yourself.
- Be the best you can be.
- Be an inspiration to yourself.
- Encourage and support yourself.
- Understand yourself.
- Forgive yourself.
- Know your values.
- Develop your passion.
- Set your personal goals.
- Live by contributing to others.

...that's how you will find your purpose in life!

Summary

- Make a positive difference to others and it can produce a strong sense of happiness and contentment.

- Understand what is most important to you and find a way to live a life being true to this and yourself.

- Everything you do in life counts, everything, every little thing no matter how small.

- When you get it wrong – don't feel bad, give yourself a break and know that learning the lesson is more important.

- Don't give in to negativity and feel helpless, take action to make it change, stay solution focused.

- Imagine your life 10 years from now and this will motivate you to do things differently today.

- Reading uplifting books and inspiring biographies helps you to connect to your own dreams and aspirations.

- Knowing what you value in life and living those values, has a positive effect on you and those around you.

- Develop your passion in life; often the thing you fear the most is your heart's deepest desire.

- Finding a way to contribute in some way to other people, provides a great sense of gratitude from others and happiness in the knowledge you are doing good.

- Reflect on the achievements in your life already.

- Be loving to yourself and others. It produces forgiveness and respect.

Recommended reading

Oh, the Places You'll Go!
by Dr Seuss
ISBN 978-0-679805-27-4

The Happiness Plan
by Carmel McConnell
ISBN 978-0-273711-78-0

Why talk to a Guru? When you can whisper to a Horse
by Paul Hunting
ISBN 978-1-905399-14-7

Feel the Fear and Do It Anyway
by Susan Jeffers
ISBN 978-0-091907-07-5

Embracing Uncertainty
by Susan Jeffers
ISBN 978-0-312325-83-1

The Power of Now
by Eckhart Tolle
ISBN 978-0-340733-50-9

Awaken the Giant Within
by Anthony Robbins
ISBN 978-0-743409-38-4

The Road Less Travelled
by M. Scott Peck
ISBN 978-0-099727-40-8

Further Along the Road Less Travelled
by M. Scott Peck
ISBN 978-0-671015-81-7

The Greatest Personal Success Tips in the World
by Brian Larcher
ISBN 978-1-905151-71-4

The Yellow Book
by Richard Wilkins
ISBN 978-0-952819-81-3

Living from the Inside Out
by Jean-Marie Hamel
ISBN 978-1-400052-74-5

My Life Tree
by Claus Moller
ISBN 978-8-789264-70-7

Getting Things Done
by David Allen
ISBN 978-0-142000-28-1

The Inner Voice of Love
Henri J M Nouwen
ISBN 978-0-385483-48-3

The Little Book of Confidence
Susan Jeffers
ISBN 978-0-974577-64-7

A space for your thoughts

....
....
....
....
....
....
....
....
....
....
....
....
....
....
....
....
....
....
....

Index

'The Greatest Tips in the World' books

Sex Tips
ISBN 978-1-905151-74-5

Travel Tips
ISBN 978-1-905151-73-8

Slimming & Healthy Living Tips
ISBN 978-1-905151-31-8

Wedding Tips
ISBN 978-1-905151-27-1

Tax Tips
ISBN 978-1-905151-43-1

Pet Recipe books

The Greatest Feline Feasts in the World
ISBN 978-1-905151-50-9

The Greatest Doggie Dinners in the World
ISBN 978-1-905151-51-6

'The Greatest in the World' DVDs

The Greatest in the World – Gardening Tips

The Greatest in the World – Yoga Tips

The Greatest in the World – Cat & Kitten Tips

The Greatest in the World – Dog & Puppy Tips

For more information about currently available
and forthcoming book and DVD titles please visit:

www.thegreatestintheworld.com

or write to:

The Greatest in the World Ltd
PO Box 3182
Stratford-upon-Avon
Warwickshire CV37 7XW
United Kingdom

Tel / Fax: +44(0)1789 299616
Email: info@thegreatestintheworld.com

The author

Simone Ryder is a professional life coach and trainer. She discovered the benefits of life coaching many years ago and has applied these techniques and principles of self-discovery to her own life, improving her well-being, confidence and happiness. Simone is passionate and dedicated to motivating others to be their best and has inspired hundreds of people to change their lives for the better, helping them to find their own passion and achieve the happiness and results they really want out of life.

Simone's own company, Life Management UK Ltd, provides e-learning and individual life management coaching and specialist well-being and self empowerment training to companies who want to reduce the risk of work-related stress to their employees and develop a better work-life balance within their organisation.

Simone keeps herself fit and healthy by practising Ashtanga Yoga and running marathons, whilst balancing her work, home and life with the two most important and motivating people in her life, her daughters Danielle and Christine.

www.simoneryder.com